Praise for The Integrated Entrepreneur

"*The Integrated Entrepreneur* will make you stop and think about all the ways you can integrate your personal and professional lives. Great ideas you can use today."
- Thomas D. Lennox, President DIB Brands, LLC; Pelotonia, Chief Executive Officer Emeritus and Brand Founder

"Randy has helped hundreds of entrepreneurs improve their lives, find success, and achieve true inner happiness. Every entrepreneur should add *The Integrated Entrepreneur* to their reading list."
- Sonny Balani, CEO, Balani Custom Clothiers

"Being a first generation entrepreneur (FGE) is the hardest challenge I have faced. As a former college football player and world champion powerlifter, I am no stranger to figuring out how to be the best at what I do. Randy has been essential in my success and *The Integrated Entrepreneur* is the definitive playbook for FGE's struggling to find happiness in their business and personal lives."
- JL Holdsworth, Founder of Reflexive Performance Reset & The Spot Athletics

"Like most entrepreneurs, I've often thought I was the smartest person in the room ... then I met Randy Gerber (also not the smartest in the room). However, *The Integrated Entrepreneur* will challenge you to not only rethink, but truly question how you currently approach both work and life. Randy's philosophy of fully integrating the two is a realistic way to achieve overall happiness and business success ... empowering you to be one of the smarter, and happier people in the room."
- Troy Allen, Chief Entertainment Officer, Rise Brands

"*The Integrated Entrepreneur* is a timely solution to the struggles every entrepreneur faces with the relationships in their lives. I have never met a financial advisor with the level of insight and intuitiveness that Randy has when it comes to building and running a business. It's really the perfect combination of financial and business advice and counsel.

- David P. Meyer, Esq. Managing Principal,
Meyer Wilson Co. LPA

THE INTEGRATED ENTREPRENEUR

ACHIEVING HAPPINESS IN RELATIONSHIPS, BUSINESS & LIFE

RANDALL T. GERBER

Published by Author Academy Elite
PO Box 43, Powell, OH 43035
www.AuthorAcademyElite.com

Identifiers:
LCCN: 2020907639
ISBN: 978-1-64746-248-2 (paperback)
ISBN: 978-1-64746-249-9 (hardback)
ISBN: 978-1-64746-250-5 (ebook)

Available in paperback, hardback, and e-book

Dedication for *The Integrated Entrepreneur*

This book is for all first-generation entrepreneurs in the world who think no one "gets it."

Much of this book was written from my personal experiences, so I'd like to thank my wife Emily; children, Zoe, Nikko and George; and my closest friends for their ongoing love and support.

A special thank you to our clients who have opened their lives to us, and allowed us to see the real challenges of first-generation entrepreneurs. Without these insights, this book would not have been possible.

TABLE OF CONTENTS

Part One: The First-Generation Entrepreneur—A Rare Bird, Indeed

Part Two: Integrating Through the Stages of Business Success

Part Three: Relationship and Business Integration for First-Generation Entrepreneurs

ACKNOWLEDGMENTS

Those of you who have known me for a long time know this book has been years in the making—many, many years in the making! I'd like to begin by thanking the people who helped get my ideas and words to paper. This includes Sarah Hackley, Kim Younkin, Kirstin Hamilton and Laurie Zinn. Without your hard work, it would still be an unfinished file on my computer, or who knows where!

The premise of this book is largely inspired by my own experience as a first-generation entrepreneur. Former generations—such as that of my parents— traditionally got jobs, worked hard, and did their best to solve problems using brute force. My generation and the generations after mine knew there was a better way. We solve our problems differently. We know we can make choices, and do our best to live a life where we can have our cake and eat it too. Watching other entrepreneurs take ownership of their lives and successfully use integration and planned experience sharing has been a great inspiration to me.

Drafts of this book have crossed many desks over the years. I'm grateful to each Gerber team member, past and present, for your ideas, suggestions and contributions. Each of you put a stamp on it in one way, shape or form, and it wouldn't be what it is today without your input.

I'd like to thank our clients for being vulnerable and allowing us an inside look at your lives, your challenges and your victories. This book would be impossible without you!

Thank you to my tribe at EO—specifically my FWF and my Visionaries forum—for lending your perspectives and insights, and letting me bounce ideas off of you. You've had a huge impact on this book in many respects.

Most importantly, I'd like to thank my wife, Emily and our children Zoe, Nikko and George. I am the luckiest person in the world to have you as my family. Your unconditional love and support mean the world to me. I know I have had my ups and downs as a spouse and a parent in our relationships; just know that every day I am trying to be the best spouse and parent I can be.

Quality time with family is the true reason and motivation behind this book. It starts with my mom and step dad, who from the time I was a pain in the ass kid were an engaged, supportive and positive presence in my life. I learned the value of family from their example. As a result of my parents' separation and subsequent divorce, I knew I wanted to be active, engaged, loving and loved husband while simultaneously being active and present in my own kids' lives. From the beginning of my marriage with Emily through raising our children, I've worked tirelessly to grow these relationships and make memorable experiences while running a business. I know I haven't been perfect, but my intention and effort were there, and will continue to be there for the rest of my life.

Inspired by all of the people mentioned above, I hope the insights and experiences that are spilled onto the following pages can help other first-generation entrepreneurs have the best of all worlds: to not just be successful in business, but to be successful at integrating your relationships, business and life.

INTRODUCTION

As I was growing up, my grandfather always gave me advice on how to live a rich, full and happy life. I vividly remember how he described the path to get there: He told me I should go to school, get good grades, get a good job with benefits, find someone to share my life with, buy a house, start a family, and work hard until retirement. While I wanted many of those things my grandfather described and I wanted to live a life as rich and full as his, I knew my path to get there was different. I knew I needed to do it on my own terms and with my own rules. And I've since learned that I'm not alone.

For about two percent of us, following someone else's rules is not an option. We want to live life on our own terms and schedules. We want to create, not produce; and we want the years we have to be defined by the growth and flourishing of our ideas. This small but powerful subset of the population is you and I—the nation's entrepreneurs.

Within this unique group, there exists an even smaller segment that has fought—often against their own logical beliefs, and the advice of friends and family—to fulfill their dream. They, like me, are first-generation entrepreneurs (FGE). They're the people who had an idea that grew into a dream and eventually into a business—successful or not. Owning and operating what they personally created, first-generation entrepreneurs may be perceived as odd and are often misunderstood for one very big reason: they make their own rules.

I started my professional service firm in Columbus, Ohio right after I graduated from The Ohio State University in 1990. While most everyone else in my life settled into a nine-to-five schedule working a good job with steady pay and stable benefits, I struck out on my own, trying to find clients in a city where I knew practically no one outside of my fraternity brothers. During my first year of business, I made $12,000 and took four weeks of vacation to fish, attend weddings, and visit wine country. I buried myself in debt. Some people thought it was a pretty dumb idea to take time away from work to experience life while spending the little money I made *and* incurring debt. Little did I know I was on to something transformational. The second year was similar, but I made $28,000 and for the first time in my life, I spent weeks skiing out West. By my third year of business, I made $70,000, developed a critical relationship that led to a client acquisition and realized that this little business of mine didn't have to be so little.

Now, more than twenty years later, the decision I made at age 22 to give "going it alone" a shot—a decision my mother didn't understand and many others didn't approve of—has paid off. The firm I founded in 1991 with a college degree and a whole lot of hope has survived and thrived during two recessions, a more than 20-year marriage to my wife, Emily, and the birth of our three children. The firm has expanded from me working relentlessly and alone for only five figures per year to a team of 16 that generates millions in revenue annually.

My story is unique to almost everyone—everyone, that is, except the first-generation entrepreneur. At one point, we all made the decision to just accept that everyone we know and love thinks we're a little bit crazy for believing in our dream and actually going for it. During the tough times, they told us to go get a real job. During the good times, they told us to count our blessings. And now, in whatever stage you're in with your business—good or bad, just launching, or nearing retirement—they probably still consider any news from your business with a bit of skepticism.

So why do they question your choice to be an entrepreneur? Trust me, it's not that they don't love you or doubt your abilities. It's never that. The truth is simple. They just don't understand. And why should they? You're an entrepreneur, which means you're acquiring

> Entrepreneurs don't conform to the rules of the rest of the business world because those rules just don't fit.

your own clients or customers, keeping crazy hours, taking economic risks and placing higher-than-normal expectations on yourself. Entrepreneurs don't conform to the rules of the rest of the business world because those rules just don't fit. Therefore, you buck societal trends, social norms and the backward glances of your family and friends to create your own set of rules—rules that are right for you.

These rules mean that you manage your time differently (or try to anyway); your successes and failures at the office aren't just career defining, they're life defining; your life outside of work is impacted by every ebb and flow of your business; your business relationships often dictate your personal relationships and vice versa; and more often than you would like, the financial state of your business determines what's left for your personal life.

All of this, coupled with the stress and responsibility of founding, managing and running a business often leaves the FGE feeling tired, overloaded and stretched too thin. In fact, that's probably why you've picked up this book: you're looking for someone who understands your situation and can help you to not just simply get through it, but also learn how to lessen or eliminate the relentless, nagging pull from your many responsibilities.

I wrote this book because I was in a very tough place in the late 1990s (like you might have been at some point or are now). My business was doing well and needed more and more of my time and attention, I had recently gotten married and purchased a house, and Emily and I were trying to manage our social lives along with our desire to start a family and still focus on our careers. The weight of it all began to place a strain on my business, my marriage and my friendships. Sound familiar?

In an attempt to figure out what could be sacrificed, I realized none of it could. The business was and is our financial security and my creative lifeline. Emily is the love of my life, and building a life and starting a family with her was all I'd ever wanted. Our friendships with others kept us young, fun and interesting (and they still do). I realized that if I could just find a way to integrate my life … if all the things I loved could support—not compete—with one another, then I could live one cohesive life instead of having a work life in opposition to my social and personal lives.

That small thought has changed how I do everything and it's what this book aims to help you do with *your* life. My goal is to help you understand that first-generation entrepreneurs are different in many ways from the rest of the population, and for this reason, they must live deliberately. I've identified five key stages first-generation entrepreneurs go through, the challenges they face in each stage and how they can overcome those challenges. I'll take you through all the stages of my own business since 1991 and show you how I've tried to live differently. I'll also provide suggestions and guidance for maintaining relationships with the key people in your life—your spouse, children, parents and friends—all those who are on this journey with you. My hope is that you'll take away something of benefit as you create your best self and build a successful business.

As first-generation entrepreneurs, we strive to be the best at everything—if we didn't, we couldn't have achieved all that we have. However, this constant need to be the best spouse, parent, friend, employer, child and whatever other role you may hold is exhausting. You can't do everything all of the time, but you can do your best to live the life you want while fulfilling all the important roles you play in life and in the world you've created around you.

PART ONE
THE FIRST-
GENERATION
ENTREPRENEUR—A
RARE BIRD, INDEED

1
HOW ENTREPRENEURS ARE DIFFERENT

We Know WHY

IN 2009, I read Simon Sinek's *Start with Why,*[1] a book that resonated so deeply with me that I gave a copy to each member of my team and also to countless others. As a matter of process, we keep many copies of this book in our office to give to prospective clients to read before they hire us. You see, for a while, I had been trying to identify whatever "it" is that makes me who I am, and what makes my team who they are. In Sinek's book, I found my answer. Sinek believes that success isn't found in *what* you do, but rather in *why* you do it. He calls this your "WHY." I called it the word I'd been looking for.

My personal WHY and the WHY of my professional service firm, Gerber, LLC, is to be a part of the innovation process that first-generation entrepreneurs go through in life. We act as their launch pad for ideas and aspirations; give them guidance for integrating and achieving their life, business, and financial goals; and provide inspiration for paying their success forward. We feel as strongly and passionately about this process with both new and established entrepreneurs. As we see it, identifying your WHY creates better lives and businesses and if we can play even a small part in that, then we've succeeded.

We knew as early as 2003 that we wanted to focus everything we did almost entirely around our niche. You know the place. It's where you find yourself most challenged and loving every minute of it. For us, we're in that place when working with first-generation entrepreneurs. Finally in 2011, all of the economic and timing stars aligned and we decided to overhaul our look, location and even the way we do things. We refined what we could, reinvented what we couldn't change, and threw out the rest to support our company WHY.

I've always said I like working with entrepreneurs because **they think differently**—and I realized I think differently too. Thanks to a study conducted by Saras Sarasvathy in 2001 called "What Makes Entrepreneurs Entrepreneurial?"[2] we know how entrepreneurs think differently from corporate leaders and professional managers.

The author says: "Entrepreneurs are entrepreneurial because … they believe in a yet-to-be-made future that can substantially be shaped by human action and they realize that to the extent that human action can control the future, they need not expend energies trying to predict it."

One of the positive byproducts of FGEs is that they are job creators and good for America. The 2018 Global Entrepreneur Indicator,[3] prepared by the Entrepreneur's Organization, found that 57 percent of entrepreneurs created new full-time jobs during the first six months of 2018, and 66 percent of entrepreneurs expected to create jobs in the last six months of 2018. A February 2017 article in Fortune magazine cited research from the Bureau of Labor Statistics, which reported that since 2014, the number of self-employed people in the US grew by nearly 150,000 to 8,751,000. This was up from 8,602,000 at the end of 2016.[4] With these trending statistics, we consider ourselves in pretty good company.

In addition to being job creators, we work with first-generation entrepreneurs because they're the first, they're visionaries, they think differently, and they're a ton of fun.

FGEs are the First

Maybe they're not the first ones to do it, but first-generation entrepreneurs are certainly the first ones to do it their way. Steve Jobs, the late co-founder and CEO of Apple, said, "Your time is limited, so don't waste it living someone else's life. And most important, have the courage to follow your heart and intuition. They somehow already know what you truly want to become."[5] First-generation entrepreneurs are the courageous ones Jobs was talking about. They've founded businesses, defended their views, and lived the life they've wanted—and we think that's admirable.

> Maybe they're not the first ones to do it, but first-generation entrepreneurs are certainly the first to do it their own way.

As an FGE, one of the first things you'll need to do is identify your own unique set of core values. These core values serve as guiding principles that define who you are as a company and who you are as people. We've identified our unique set of core values at Gerber and they are:

1. Be present and positive

2. Bold pursuit of excellence

3. Live and breathe entrepreneurship

4. Have a healthy sense of urgency

Our core values give us a set of boundaries to live our WHY. They help us stay focused on what we want to do and where we want to go. You know your WHY, too, even if you haven't put it into words yet.

FGEs are Visionary

FGEs see what can be and they make it happen, not only for themselves, but for us all. No other segment of the population is as vital to local, regional, and national economies as entrepreneurs. Through our ambition and creative visions, we generate wealth, create jobs, and grow economies. We imagine, redesign, and revitalize industries. We also transform our own lives, our employees' lives and eventually, entire societies through what we create—both inside and outside of the workplace. Most importantly, we possess a can-do attitude that inspires the people around us. This can-do attitude is rooted in American values. Your business—just like this country—was founded on the idea that "there must be a better way."

Americans are leading nations when it comes to starting a business, as our capital markets are the "deepest and most liquid in the world."[6] Our investors use capital to drive innovation, economic growth and job creation. We embrace entrepreneurs, which is why so many companies come here to raise capital, grow their business and/or go public. Without entrepreneurs, we'd grow slower and produce less. We'd also create far fewer jobs. According to a 2015 article from the Ewing Marion Kauffman Foundation, an organization dedicated to creating educational and entrepreneurial opportunities for everyone, companies less than one year old have created an average of 1.5 million jobs per year over the past three decades.[7] This is the fuel of the American economic engine.

Productivity is and always has been driven by entrepreneurial activities, and its increase generates local, regional, and national wealth. High productivity growth generally molds a country into a worldwide exporter (e.g., the U.S., China, India), and major exporters produce greater profits and better returns for investors. In the 19th century, for example, Cyrus McCormick

Sr.'s horse-drawn mechanical reaper allowed U.S. farmers to double their production rates and thus established the U.S. as an agricultural superpower.[8]

Also in the 19th century, Andrew Carnegie's efficient improvements to the steel industry dramatically increased the ability of the U.S. to produce steel. By 1889, Carnegie Steel Corporation was the largest of its kind in the world.[9] More recently, Steve Wozniak and Steve Jobs revolutionized desktop computing with their Mac OS. The switch from a C: prompt operating system to a user-friendly personal computer transformed the workplace and boosted individual productivity. The evolution of Apple's products has had a profound impact on several different industries that have radically altered the way the world communicates and consumes information.[10]

When entrepreneurs act out their dreams, there's no limit to what they can achieve, whether it's transforming an industry or creating an entirely new way of life. Carl J. Schramm, former president of the Kauffman Foundation, credits entrepreneurship as the secret that has led the American economy to be the strongest in the world.[11]

Consider Edison's electric light bulb, Rockefeller's Standard Oil refineries, Henry Ford's "affordable automobile," George Eastman's Kodak film roll, Hershey's chocolates, Asa Candler's Coca Cola, and Steve Jobs' "I" revolution. Out of these entrepreneur's dreams and decisions to take risks came an entirely new way of life both in the U.S. and abroad.

Today, we can effortlessly find information online by "googling" it, share documents and spreadsheets worldwide with Microsoft Office, and keep up with our friends and families all over the world on Facebook, Instagram, Facetime and Skype. We do all this on iPhones, iPads, and tablets that weigh as little as several ounces to no more than a few pounds thanks to the insight, vision, and risk tolerance of entrepreneurs. Without them, our current way of life would not exist.

Battelle, the nation's leading research institute, fuels entrepreneurism and innovation. It has made significant societal and economic impacts in the areas of science, technology, and manufacturing in the oil and gas industry, among others. They've developed vaccines and therapeutics for infectious diseases, built specialized tactical equipment for military troops, and improved products in our everyday lives like roofing shingles, cruise control, microwave dishes and even adhesives to keep our Oreos fresh.

Tesla is making a worldwide impact with the development of commercially viable electric cars and batteries for storing solar-generated power. Who would have ever thought we'd have the option to plug in and charge our vehicles at night—much like we do our phones and laptops?

In addition to worldwide change, we also create new ways of life on a much smaller scale: the workplace. SAS Institute, Inc., a thriving software business founded in 1976, is an example of how entrepreneurs can dramatically improve the quality of their employees' lives simply by following their dreams and critically assessing the impact of their employees on their bottom lines. With $3.2 billion in revenues in 2016, SAS's co-founder and CEO Dr. James "Jim" Goodnight has often been quoted, saying that 95 percent of his assets "drive out the gate every evening," and that it is his "job to maintain a work environment that keeps those people coming back every morning."[12]

For over 40 years, the company has experienced solid, unbroken growth under its original leadership. Though it has about 14,000 employees, it has never had a single layoff. Both its employees and its founders generally report a happy integration of work and life. How have the founders accomplished such amazing success?

As Goodnight says, "software is a people business," and its biggest assets are its employees. Keep them happy, and they'll work harder, produce more and stick around longer, he advocates. With that in mind, Goodnight and his co-founders Anthony Barr, John Sall, and Jane Helwig created a corporate headquarters often described as a "Corporate Shangri La." One step on the grounds and it's easy to see why the employees would want to keep coming back day after day.

The property sits on 140 acres and includes an on-site health care center (used by 90 percent of SAS's employees) staffed with over 50 doctors, nurses, and medical professionals; an indoor gym with cardio equipment; indoor basketball and racquetball courts; soccer fields; football fields; a jogging track; a meditation garden; and a 75-foot indoor pool. There's also a nail and hair salon, two daycare centers for children under five, and a work/life building that provides help with financial planning, adoption needs, and more. The cafeteria serves up company-subsidized gourmet lunches, and employees can often be seen having lunch with their spouses and children. Art and sculptures created by the on-site artist fill the halls.

Fortune magazine has listed SAS as one of the 100 Best Companies to Work For every year since 1997.[13] The company's employees are happy, loyal, and productive—all of which has been crucial to SAS's international success. The co-founders are an inspiration and serve as a perfect example of what's possible when entrepreneurs combine a profit motive with vision, innovation, and generosity.

Of course, creating that kind of change isn't easy. In fact, nothing about being an entrepreneur is easy. According to the Bureau of Labor Statistics, 20 percent of small businesses fail in the first year and 30 percent fail in their second year.[14] Long-term success is even less likely. Entrepreneur magazine cites a study that reports a 50 percent failure rate of all U.S. companies after five years; and over 70 percent failure rate after 10 years.[15]

Those are daunting odds—to anyone, that is, except the first-generation entrepreneur.

FGEs Think Differently

First-generation entrepreneurs aren't interested in easy. We're interested in achievement, growing, and pushing the limits. We're interested in innovation, exploration and most importantly, we're interested in FUN! We believe we can live life a better way than by working for "the man." We want to lead better lives, be better spouses and raise better kids. We want to create experiences that are unique, innovative and all about full engagement. Most notably, we want success and we're pretty sure we're going to attain it. We think differently than non-entrepreneurs.

Entrepreneurs not only want success, we expect it. Therefore we must put ourselves in a position to win. But how? Optimism and passion aside, what is it that drives the success of those 80 percent of businesses who make it to their second year? The 50 percent who make it to the fifth year? Or the 30 percent of businesses who make it to their 10th year?

It comes down to hard work, persistence, and determination. But, sometimes, no matter how much effort you put in, your success will come down to luck. As entrepreneurs, we will encounter both good luck and bad luck during our business's lifetime, but it's how we handle that luck that really matters. As your business evolves and you mature as an entrepreneur, you will be more effective in your ability to manage bad luck, and more opportunistic when good luck presents itself.

Thankfully, though, success isn't *all* luck. There are a number of components to success that can be studied, learned, and implemented in order to increase your chances of making it to that 10-year mark, particularly when it comes to interacting with the people around you. As author John C. Maxwell writes, "The greatest skill needed for success is the ability to get along with other people … Your relationships make you or they break you."[16]

Maxwell's right. That's why this book is designed to encourage you, the first-generation entrepreneur, to explore, consider, and—in some cases—recreate your relationships with those around you: your spouse, your children, your parents, and your closest friends. This book also discusses how your relationships with others will impact and be impacted by your relationship with your business, and how those interactions will change as your business grows and evolves. Because nothing exists in isolation, this book will also encourage you to use proactive, planned experience sharing to integrate your relationships in a way that enables you to experience the utmost satisfaction in all areas of your life.

First generation entrepreneurs think about the world differently than everybody else. We believe there is a better way. Too often though, entrepreneurs limit that thinking to their businesses, when in reality, that type of thinking can make us better spouses, parents, friends, siblings and children. We simply have to let the creative ways we think about our businesses transcend to the way we think about all of the relationships in our lives. I call this planned experience sharing, and we'll discuss it more throughout this book.

It takes a certain kind of person to shun stability, risk failure and financial insecurity, and welcome bouts of failure—even temporarily. It's not a move many people make. It's not a move that many people can even understand. (Let that thought linger: you are a rare, special person.) And if you don't believe me on this, remember: "Entrepreneurship is living a few years of your life like most people won't, so that you can spend the rest of your life like most people can't."[17]

Entrepreneurs vs. Non-Entrepreneurs

Someone on the street, if asked, might say entrepreneurs are different by degree: that we possess more energy, more optimism, and more ambition than most people. We entrepreneurs tend to say we just don't like the status quo and think our way is better. In fact, the differences between entrepreneurs and non-entrepreneurs are much subtler than believed. Personality research conducted over the past sixty years has sought to illuminate those differences and it can tell us a lot about what makes entrepreneurs successful. It can also aid the aspiring entrepreneur in understanding the road that lies ahead.[18]

Entrepreneurs expect success—and we're willing to risk much more than other people to get it. We approach our work with a fervor and intensity that most people can't match, and we're more than willing to make sacrifices—sometimes extreme sacrifices—for the sake of our mission. That doesn't mean we crave risk more than other people. In fact, according to recent research, entrepreneurs are no more outgoing, spontaneous, risk-tolerant, ruthless or motivated by money than other people. We are, however, more likely to have a high self-efficacy—a belief in ourselves that we can achieve whatever we put our minds toward achieving. And we want to do it ourselves—we often find it difficult to delegate and to trust others. You may believe that people around you do not perform as well as you, or see that their performance does not meet the expectations you have for them within the abilities you know they possess. This lack of trust in others' abilities is clearly related in part to ego, making it hard for an entrepreneur to transfer control and delegate. It's very hard to do, but many successful business owners have overcome those issues.[19]

Entrepreneurs also care much less about what others think of them, which can be a good thing. Especially in situations like handling naysayers—it's a steadfast belief in our ability to influence our success that enables us to enthusiastically barrel through negative input and to make it through the initial stages of success without succumbing to doubt.

Research has shown a marked difference between entrepreneurs and non-entrepreneurs—we have a much higher need for achievement than non-entrepreneurs.[20] We value success and we value ourselves more highly when we believe we have achieved it. A real or perceived lack of achievement can affect our self-esteem. Often with time, mini-victories lead to more confidence and bigger victories. Experience uniquely equips the entrepreneur with the tools to solve real problems much more efficiently than non-entrepreneurs.

In other words, your victories and your failures combine. If you can learn from your victories and your failures, you will become a much more effective and efficient problem solver in the future.

Oftentimes, if we achieve less, we believe we are worth less. So we are willing to sacrifice almost everything—time for ourselves, other responsibilities, even sleep—to attain our goals. Unfortunately, if we aren't careful, our intensity and our willingness to let other aspects of our lives go in order to reach that high level of achievement can easily begin to damage relationships with our spouses, our children, our friends, and even our business partners.

Successful Entrepreneurs vs. Unsuccessful Entrepreneurs

Just like there are differences between entrepreneurs and non-entrepreneurs, research shows there are clear but subtle personality differences between entrepreneurs who succeed and those who don't. According to research conducted by Carl Robinson, Ph.D., successful entrepreneurs share five personality characteristics: emotional intelligence, optimism, tolerance for frustration, tolerance for criticism, and self-control.[21] Understanding these differences and learning how they attribute to success can help aspiring or struggling entrepreneurs get back on the track.

Successful entrepreneurs have insight into people (emotional intelligence), which enables them to know what people want and need, sell the product or service that fits that need and cultivate relationships with customers/clients, partners, etc. Importantly, successful entrepreneurs are able to manage their emotions while under intense stress (self-control) without unfairly putting pressure on employees, partners, clients or customers. Since entrepreneurialism is often exceptionally stressful, this ability to control emotions in the face of adversity is key for an aspiring entrepreneur to become successful. It isn't just the way entrepreneurs approach success that makes them different. It's also the way they view failure.

In the book "Failing Forward," John C. Maxwell says that success doesn't come from family background, wealth, opportunity, integrity or the absence of hardship. Rather, he says, "The difference between average people and achieving people is their perception of and response to failure." First-generation entrepreneurs don't view their failures as failures, they view their failures as opportunities to learn from their mistakes and gain the knowledge necessary to do it better the next time around.

Most people are taught to avoid failure. Most people learn to fear mistakes. Most people dread "looking stupid." We can't learn if we don't make mistakes. It is the process of recognizing a mistake, acknowledging it, and figuring out how to correct it that propels us through higher and tougher experiences.

Since we entrepreneurs need more achievement to be happy than other people, we're going to have to risk more and make more mistakes to get there. FGEs quickly learn mistakes are opportunities—experiences that usually illuminate the problem to create a better way. As your experience evolves as a FGE, you will often look forward to the mistakes your company makes in order to accelerate the learning curve. Bill Gates, Michael Dell, Warren Buffett, and Mark Zuckerberg didn't get where they are by doing everything perfectly the first time around. We have to fail in order to succeed. It's part of the process.

Optimism is a critical component of failing gracefully. Since they believe they will be successful, these entrepreneurs often forge on through adversity, even when faced with a temporary failure. As I'll discuss further in this book, temporary failures (for instance, the loss of a key employee or client, or a failed product line) can become permanent if the entrepreneur doesn't know how to consider the problem, overcome it and persevere. Successful entrepreneurs believe they will overcome temporary failures and thrive because of them.

Successful entrepreneurs also have a high tolerance for frustration and criticism, which really goes back to the strong self-efficacy discussed earlier. We entrepreneurs believe in ourselves and that enables us to withstand naysayers. It also helps us manage the immense stresses and frustrations that come from starting and running a business.

We Believe in Our Own Success

Entrepreneurism isn't easy. I've already discussed the myriad ways it makes life more difficult, especially at first—we lack sleep, sex, exercise, time for ourselves, time for our families, and often in the beginning, money. Despite all this, we want to work for ourselves. We want to see our ideas come to fruition. We believe in our hearts that there is a better way. We often can't think of anything else. And, most importantly, we believe we will succeed.

It is this belief in our own success that allows us to make the sacrifices we're required to make for the sake of the business. We can handle the daily frustrations and stresses. Our self-efficacy pushes us through.

To become a lasting success, to become one of the one in 10,000 businesses that make it ten years, we'll think differently, because that's who we are.

2
WHY INTEGRATE?

TIME IS ONE of the most precious resources for us all, and lack of it is one of the most common problems entrepreneurs face. There never seems to be enough time. Not for family. Not for friends. Not for clients or the everyday details of running a business. And we certainly never seem to have enough for ourselves. A healthy work-life relationship is the entrepreneur's holy grail. Most of us struggle to find it, and feel guilty as a result.

This is because the traditional idea of work-life (where work is from seven to seven, or five to five, or 10 to five or later; and life is everything else) doesn't work for first-generation entrepreneurs. Particularly in the early start-up years, working a limited number of hours doesn't seem like an option. There are things to sell, customers to woo, cash flow to manage, employees to hire and fire, and the endless list goes on. Things that should be non-negotiable—time with our kids or spouse, healthy meals, exercise, sex, and sleep—start to fall victim to other "more pressing" matters, all in the name of the business.

Research shows that U.S. adults are sleeping over an hour less per night than they did in the 1940s.[22] This is likely due to the rise in workplace productivity demands and the increasing numbers of entrepreneurs who work out of their homes. Both scenarios translate into having more to do in fewer hours. Not getting enough sleep can lead to a variety of health problems, including weight gain, difficulties with hormonal regulation, higher stress levels and cardiovascular disease. And less sleep means less energy, concentration and focus.

In addition to the health problems associated with lack of sleep, a report from the Whitehall II Study, published in the American Journal of Epidemiology indicates that middle-aged people who work long hours show increased rates of cognitive decline.[23]

An out of whack work-life relationship can result in untreated and excessive chronic stress, which numerous studies have linked to problems with cognition, increased risk levels for cardiovascular disease, cancer, dementia, and problems with your spouse, family and friends. I recommend reading *Why Zebras Don't Get Ulcers* by Robert Sapolsky for a detailed description of the serious adverse health effects of chronic stress.[24]

Your body is like a fine-tuned engine and when it doesn't have the proper fuel, sleep, exercise and diet, you can't perform at your highest level. In the beginning stages of business, the first-generation entrepreneur needs every advantage possible. While it may seem like you have to work 24 hours a day to keep up with your ever-expanding list of things to do, those extra hours don't add any additional value to your company. You may answer more emails, make more calls and file more paper if you work through dinner, but you're unlikely to think any more creatively or accomplish goal-oriented tasks that translate into a more sustainable business long-term. The path of least resistance is to simply work more. However, you need to think differently.

Thinking differently means adopting strategies and priorities that allow you to take care of yourself so you can take care of your business. Here are a few ways we've advised our clients to manage their ever-increasing workload:

- Focus only on what will really move you forward. Remember: working longer isn't necessarily working smarter. Carefully consider and catalog the essential tasks you must do and those that you can delegate or simply ignore in order to maximize your efforts, energy and supreme skills in the areas that matter most.

- Develop a written plan on paper, on your laptop, or in Google Docs—whichever is more comfortable for you. The sheer act of putting your plan in writing commits you to it, as well as makes you more thoughtful. Business plan templates and guidelines are available for download from SCORE (Service Corps of Retired Executives), the U.S. Small Business Administration, and Entrepreneur Media, Inc.[25] Once you've created your plan, develop a rhythm to routinely and systemically review and tweak to ensure the plan becomes reality.

- Block time away from the day-to-day pressures and distractions to observe your business through a different lens. Schedule time away from the office to give your mind and body the freedom to think, be creative and relax. You may view the time away as a loss, when really it is the best investment you can make in yourself and your business. If you train yourself to take time away on a regular schedule, your business will thrive, your marriage will be happier, and you can be healthier in all aspects of your life.

- Make exercise a part of your daily routine. This doesn't necessarily mean you have to run a marathon or train for the Ironman. Entrepreneur magazine said it's not important where you exercise, how you exercise or even how long you exercise.[26] What really matters is that you just take the time to do it. Exercise reduces stress, has undeniable health benefits and keeps your brain sharp.

- If you enjoy a cocktail at a conference or networking event, attend your business' weekly happy hour, or unwind at the end of a long day with a cold beer or a glass of wine, you are not alone. As entrepreneurs, we often include alcohol when we need to blow off steam, bond with clients or customers, or celebrate a business victory. As with anything else in life, moderation is key, and it can be helpful to establish guidelines. Too much of this type of fun can actually reduce your productivity, as well as take a toll on your overall health. I bring this up because overworked entrepreneurs are especially at risk. Studies show there is a connection between a heavy workload and alcohol use, and those who work longer hours are 11 percent more likely to engage in risky alcohol consumption.[27]

Like any other resource, your energy is a precious and limited commodity. Pressing yourself longer, harder and faster may make your to-do list look good today, but it will likely lead to exhaustion and burnout. What's worse, when you exhaust yourself every day, you'll have zero energy to spend on strategy and business growth. How do you work less, conserve energy, and spend your time in ways that make you, your family and your business thrive?

You integrate.

Integration is identifying the things that you are the best at doing in your business, your home and your personal life, and making a conscious decision to merge them together whenever possible. For example, if you need to take a business trip, you could bring your family with you for a vacation or weekend getaway. One day of the trip would be reserved to meet with a customer or attend a conference while your family relaxes by the pool and the remaining days would be spent sightseeing, visiting

> Integration is identifying the things that you are best at doing in your business, your home and your personal life, and making the conscious decision to merge them together whenever possible.

with friends that live in the area, or just enjoying some family bonding time in a different city.

Integrating is different from balance, a word that is frequently thrown at busy entrepreneurs as the definitive solution to managing hectic work and home lives. Consider for a moment what the word "balancing" brings to your mind. A seesaw? A tightrope walker? A server with a tray piled high with plates? Whatever the image, it likely depicts something precarious, a scene that could easily—with a small amount of wind or extra weight or change in speed—come crashing down around the person attempting to maintain that balance.

Balance is not easy. In fact, it's typically stressful and disappointing because it requires that you add or take away from your true goal in order to remain in a calm state. Many times, a lack of balance can induce guilt, which is one of the worst states of mind to operate in. So why do people strive so hard to attain it? Trying to give an equal amount of a limited resource—such as your time or energy—to complete tasks in separate areas of your life usually means none of the parts are receiving as much of you as it needs (or as much as you'd like to give). In reality, balancing alone just doesn't work. To be happier, healthier and most productive, you have to integrate the competing areas of your life into a single, comprehensive whole.

That means figuring out what's important to you, what success means to you, where you want to be in each stage of your life and what you need to do to achieve those goals. This can be difficult and one could argue that it should be difficult, if you are to do it right. Almost everyone knows what is important in their life on some level, especially entrepreneurs. The trick is to utilize deliberate tactics to successfully integrate all that is important in your life and accomplish your goals in every area of your life—not just business.

Unconditional Friends

If you reflect on your own life, you will likely find that you've had certain friends come and go over time. Whether it's your best friend from high school, your college roommate or a past colleague, these friends tend to walk in and out of your life. Consider the difference between a temporary friend who is here for the moment (for good or bad reasons) and the lifelong friend you know is there with you forever. How many "unconditional" friends do you have in your life right now? Who are the people that would be there for you through anything? Do you enjoy your time with them? Do you feel better about yourself when you're with them? Is it a "safe" environment for you? Consider what would it be like to invest your precious time only into those unconditional friends you know will invest their precious time and energy back into YOU?

Think back on the wasted energy and time you've invested over the years in relationships that didn't matter in the end. While most relationships provide new ways to grow through varied experiences and contacts, many of us invest our time and energy on dead-end relationships. Consider if you were able to have three to five "unconditional" friendships—friends who are there for you no matter what or when—and how your life would be from a time and enjoyment perspective.

While you will always have a multitude of acquaintances—and it's very important to have those people in your life—imagine what your life would look like if you deliberately placed the investment of your time, emotions and energy *only* with those few trusted and unconditional friends mentioned above versus your casual acquaintances? You'd most likely be happier, feel more secure, be less stressed, and be able to spend your time on the things and the people who matter most to you.

I feel very lucky to have several unconditional friends. One friend has been in my life for over 30 years, two friends have known me for over 25 years and other friends have been by my side for 15-20 years. The commonality among all of us is positive energy, and our friendship is fun and fulfilling, both personally and in business. In some cases, our families have spent so much time together both at home and away that my kids think the other kids are their cousins. When I think about my unconditional friends, I know that under any circumstance, they are always going to be a friend, and it's nearly impossible to imagine a scenario where that wouldn't be the case.

Having those lifelong, unconditional friends in your life adds positive energy, and feeds your curiosity and emotional intelligence. They make you happier. They don't detract from your personal or business life. They are invested in you and your family because they care about your kids, your spouse and all aspects of your life outside of business. When you have a strong unconditional friendship, it's a mutually beneficial relationship.

It's important to look for consistent behavior in people. Lifelong, unconditional friends behave like lifelong, unconditional friends and any deviation from that is a rare occurrence that can be explained away. If those occurrences begin to happen more frequently and you feel like the friendship is one-sided, that person may not be a true lifelong, unconditional friend, and you should treat the relationship as such. It doesn't mean he or she is a bad or malicious person. It just means the individual shouldn't have access to your time, brain space and emotions the way it was before.

Achieving Integration

There are as many ways to achieve integration as there are paths to success. The trick is to find the kind of integration that works for you. Imagine if you were in a professional service business and you loved to downhill ski or snowboard. Wouldn't it make sense to take ski trips with your family and clients who were also your best friends? You could do that same thing with fishing trips, baseball games, nature hikes and other similarly engaging activity.

Part of the integration process I describe throughout this book is what I like to call "planned experience sharing," and the key to its implementation is to live *deliberately*. Every decision you make should be a decision that brings you closer to where you want to be next year, five years from now, ten years from now and so on. As your business grows and evolves, and your personal priorities shift and change, you'll find that the process of integration requires you to pay a great deal of attention to both internal and external factors. While it does take time and energy, planned experience sharing—if implemented effectively—is a process that ensures you will live your life the way you want to live it and that you'll enjoy it along the way. And it also increases your business's odds of success!

Integrating your life and making deliberate choices requires you to think through some important questions:

1. What aspects of your life are most important? Family, friends, business, fitness, religion? What makes you truly happy—the happy you envision in your most private thoughts? The happy that is pure, in your deepest, innermost soul? What relationships do you want to nourish?

2. What aspects of your life are least important but still manage to suck out your energy? Which relationships are dead ends? Where do you spend time every day, week or month that you wish you could recapture?

3. Where do you want to be in your personal and professional life next week, next month, next year? What about in five years? Ten? Is this written down? Is it routinely reviewed and adjusted?

4. What do you need to do in the next 90 days and over the next year to move you closer to your five-year, ten-year, and twenty-year goals?

5. What should you stop doing now to ensure you meet these goals? What do you do now that has no impact on whether or not you reach your most important goals? Why are you doing those things?

6. How do you measure or chart your progress? Are you routinely evaluating what is really important to you? Are you proactively eliminating time spent on those people or activities in your life that won't get you where you want to be in 10 or 25 years?

If you've never considered these questions, now is the time to start. As a first-generation entrepreneur, you're most likely busier now than you have ever been before. Particularly in the beginning stages of business, there's not enough time in the day for even the most necessary of activities (eating, sleeping, exercise or sex), let alone time to watch a movie with your spouse, to help your children with their homework or to enjoy your favorite pastime with friends. With such a packed schedule, it may seem like you don't have time for this kind of planning. But your exceptionally full schedule is *exactly* why you have to start planning now, today.

If you want to fully enjoy your life and your relationships, you must make sure that every single item on your to-do list meets your goals for today and furthers your goals for the future. There are many tools available to help keep you aligned with those goals day to day. Before you enter an item on your to-do list or schedule a meeting or event, consider its purpose. How does it match your answers to the questions above? Will it help you? Your business? Your spouse? Your kids? Is it essential to your goals? Will it further or hinder your relationships with those you love?

If the item or meeting doesn't match your goals for the future, you might want to consider whether the activity is really worth doing. Perhaps you could leave that item undone for now or turn down that third networking event. Prioritizing can be difficult, but if you really take the time to consider how your actions benefit you and bring you closer to your goals, you should find it's easier to figure out whether to attend that seminar or if it's the right time to expand your business.

Considering why you do what you do will also help clarify your goals and your priorities. Why do you get out of bed in the morning? Why did you start your business? Why did you have a family? Ideally, the answers to those questions should form a coherent whole—your personal "WHY" and your business "WHY" should be in alignment. If the reason you started your business doesn't mesh with your personal priorities, you will likely find yourself constantly mired in work/life conflicts. Consider what that means for your personal and professional goals long-term. Should you keep a business that doesn't fit into your personal passions? Is there a way to align the two that maybe you haven't thought of? We'll discuss how to do this throughout this book.

Artfully integrating your life will help you avoid working longer and harder than you have to while nourishing the relationships that are important to you. It will also keep you healthier—today and in the future. A recent Wells Fargo/Gallup Small Business Index poll shows that increasing numbers of entrepreneurs don't plan to retire until their health forces them to do so.[28] If you're like them and want to work indefinitely, it is crucial that you learn the art of integration and avoid working long hours over most of your professional life.

If you want to succeed—in life as well as in business—you're going to have to embrace integration and planned experience sharing. Learning to plan deliberately and live your life mindfully means your sleep will be sounder, your body will be healthier, your mind will be more focused, and both your family and your business will be stronger. Integration is the key to your success. But it doesn't have to be difficult. Just take a few moments now to think about the questions in this chapter, and remember to reflect on your answers as you read through the rest of this book.

Then get ready: it's time to begin integrating your life through planned experience sharing.

3
PLANNED EXPERIENCE SHARING

PLANNED EXPERIENCE SHARING is one of the strongest tools an entrepreneur has for achieving success in business and in life. While many entrepreneurs expect a better quality of life for themselves and their families once their businesses become successful, most entrepreneurs don't start a business with a clear, developed plan for building the ideal work-life relationship. Creating and implementing such a plan requires tremendous passion and courage. The few bold entrepreneurs who learn to integrate their work lives with their personal lives realize a level of success and happiness that others can hardly imagine. (They also have a lot more fun along the way.)

When I first founded my business, I viewed it as a means by which to continue the party that was my college experience. Because I could set my own hours and determine my vacation time, I was able to take those four weeks each year to do what I loved. I was able to party five days a week and just have fun the other two! When others started taking my business seriously, however, I realized that I should too.

So I buckled down and began working. I worked staggering hours every week. I didn't stop having fun or seeing my friends—I just made work my top priority. That routine continued for about three years. If I wasn't at work, I was at a party with my friends or traveling somewhere. I barely slept; ate poorly, not caring about healthy eating and relaxing was not a word in my vocabulary. Miraculously though, I met Emily—the daughter of Greek immigrants who started their own business—and she understood my hectic schedule and the demands of being an entrepreneur. And she loved to have fun too. We got married and bought our first home in 1996.

It wasn't too long after when I realized something needed to change. I was stretched entirely too thin and was not taking care of myself, or the relationships I had worked so hard to build. I attended a conference that taught me I needed to work ON my business, not IN it. It also taught me that it's okay for business owners to find and take personal time. I decided to integrate all the loves of my life and focus on planning experiences that allowed me to **share** the time that I would normally **split** between my work, family, and personal lives.

I am fortunate enough to work in an industry in which my clients are my friends. And I say this in that order because it wasn't always that way. I used to have friends and family members as clients; but after a while, the "client" factor infringed on the "friend and family" factor to the point where I was happy and relieved to separate from the business relationship. I've worked hard since to develop friendships with my clients—but the professional business relationship with them comes first—and my team and I strive for excellence daily in pursuit of their goals. These clients are also my friends. We spend a lot of time together doing things each of us loves.

Skiing, golfing, clay shooting, storytelling, laughing and watching Ohio State football and basketball are just a few personal interests that I share with my clients. We discuss our businesses on the green, our marriage and other relationships at the range, and we cut loose at the same time. The thing with business owners is that we never have free time because we're always thinking about our business. This is why whenever we can combine the needs of the business with the needs of our family and self, we do.

Joining the Entrepreneurs Organization (EO)[29] has proven to be the best business decision I ever made. What started as a continuing education opportunity for me became a complete game-changer in both my personal and professional lives. My fellow entrepreneurs understand the issues I deal with as a business owner, husband, father, and friend. Given that EO is founded on the premise of providing a safe environment for sharing with no judgment from your fellow business owners, many in my network have become some of my best friends.

These are the opportunities all entrepreneurs need to embrace. Think of the things that you really love. Your spouse, your children, your business, your favorite hobby or two, and belonging to an organization are all probably going to be at the top of the list. Now look for the links between all of these things. Can you take customers to the driving range or your wife on your next business trip? How about providing your kids with a lesson in work ethic by having them help out with small jobs around the office?

You may be able to piggyback off your trade organizations' events, other networking groups, or conferences to plan activities that include both your clients and your family. If you work in manufacturing, planned experience sharing could include opportunities with your vendors, suppliers or distributors. The goal is finding the intersection of your family's passion and your business needs. The activities you choose will depend on the area of the country you live in.

For example, if you live in Boston or somewhere on the east coast where water sports are prevalent, you may get involved with power boating, sailing, or yacht clubs that have a mix of people who share your family's love of the water. If you live in Buffalo, you might find networking opportunities during summer sailboat races or winter ski clubs. Michigan offers snowmobile clubs in winter and lake activities in the summer. Most North American wines come from the west coast, so states like California, Oregon and Washington offer experiences such as wine expos, vineyard tours, and wine tasting events. Hunting, fishing, luxury sports car clubs, and countless other sports or special interest groups all provide planned experience sharing opportunities for you, your family and your clients. The key is to consider what you do for a living, where you live, and what your family loves to do. Then determine how you can combine them all in an experience that allows you to network with business associates while spending time with your family.

I prioritize and practice planned experience sharing regularly in my own life. When my family's vacation had to be changed at the last minute due to an impending hurricane, we decided to head to New York City, a destination we've visited before and my kids love. While there, we visited with one of my wife's long-time unconditional friends, my kids were front and center on the floor for the 9:30 bell ringing at the New York Stock Exchange, our sons competed against each other in a second annual self-organized steak-eating contest, and we stayed at the home of an unconditional friend of mine. I deliberately integrated everything in my life in this trip to make it a fun and productive time for my family, while also nurturing my business relationships.

Wear Fewer Hats

Planned experience sharing may take some of the spontaneity out of life, but it also removes the stress and burden that goes along with trying to wear too many hats too often. Consider all the hats you wear at the office: you are most likely CEO, CFO, HR and PR Directors, the head of sales, and occasionally,

> Planned experience sharing may take the spontaneity out of life, but it also removes the stress and burden that goes along with trying to wear too many hats to often.

janitor. What do you dislike the most about these titles and what do you love? Can you pass some of the responsibility to other team members to take some of the work off your plate and allow them to grow and develop within their career?

As an example, if you own a business that's in heavy manufacturing and the status quo is to visit your clients at their business locations, why not create a sales cycle that doesn't include you? It is common practice for the first-generation entrepreneur to be the key sales person during a business's first years. A different paradigm would be to make the investment in a professional salesperson or sales solution that keeps you off the road. Your salesperson gets the valuable experience and responsibility that he/she needs or even craves, and you get a lighter load. Everybody wins—that's a huge component of planned experience sharing.

My very first employee hire was an administrative assistant who relieved me of the mundane duties of routine paperwork, completing applications, scheduling and confirming appointments, etc. I knew I had to hire her because I was running at capacity, but it took me nearly a week to determine what I could delegate to her. After hiring many employees over the years, I've learned—and have told my clients—that the biggest expense of a new employee is no more than three months of their salary. After that, if they are good at what they do, they pay for themselves. My first administrative assistant saved me a ton of time and money in just confirming and rescheduling appointments.

It can be difficult to let go of responsibilities you've had since you started your business and you may find it helpful to invest in a business system that gives you the framework you need to do so. At Gerber, we use the Entrepreneurial Operating System (EOS),[30] a set of simple concepts and practical tools that helps us identify our core values, develop our leadership teams, and holds us accountable for our responsibilities. Using EOS, we've developed a communication rhythm and accountability chart that keeps us on task so we understand our roles, who we are accountable to and when. Our accountability chart includes an

Integrator, whose job, among other things, is to protect me from doing things that aren't productive or aren't in my area of expertise.

Wearing too many hats is actually detrimental to your business, because it prevents it from moving forward. Our accountability chart clearly defines everyone's responsibilities and ensures that no one is working over and above their capacity. With the help of EOS, we've learned to delegate responsibilities to those who have strengths in certain areas. Then, everyone is productive, performing within their own abilities and with a clear understanding of how their role impacts the rest of the organization.

I highly recommend investing in a system like EOS, Rockefeller Habits[31] or MAP Management Consulting.[32] These systems came out in the mid-1990s when there wasn't a lot of help and support for small businesses; most of us relying on networking with other entrepreneurs to determine the business practices that worked best. These systems can be expensive in terms of dollars and time, require you to have a high sales minimum to get started— and can be hard to implement within a startup. I encourage you to at least read the books, engage with the system and start the process.

Early in my career I was given a piece of advice I want to share with you. **Only do those things that you are world class at doing.** Delegate those tasks—consistently and always—that you are NOT world class at doing, that cause you stress and are time consuming simply because it's a task that's not in your wheelhouse. When you are operating at your best, you can deliberately integrate your business and personal lives, and plan those shared experiences with the people who matter most in your life.

PART TWO
INTEGRATING THROUGH THE STAGES OF BUSINESS SUCCESS

4
DEFINING SUCCESS

THIS BOOK IS not a "how to be successful in business" book, and any book for first-generation entrepreneurs should at least briefly discuss a few vitally important elements of success. In beginning to integrate your life, you must think strategically about the three main elements that I believe can increase your business's odds of making it to the second year. They are timing, idea inspiration and support network. You'll use this knowledge as you make deliberate steps toward integration in each stage of your blooming business.

Timing

Entrepreneurs who have a good sense of future trends and opportunities have greater degrees of success than other entrepreneurs. It's easy to see why entering an industry at the "right" time can make a big difference in whether or not a business succeeds. Amazingly, though, it can even make a difference in whether or not a first-generation entrepreneur's *next* business venture succeeds.

For example, a Harvard business study suggests that an entrepreneur who started a computer business in 1983—the first year that more than ten million computers were in use in the United States—would not only have a greater chance of success in their computer business than an entrepreneur who started a computer business two years later, but he or she would also have a greater chance of success in subsequent business ventures than would the other entrepreneur.[33] With odds like that, you want to make sure you start your business at the perfect (or at least near perfect) time. How?

There are at least four timing issues that need to be in alignment for your business to be a success: economical timing, technological timing, political timing and personal timing. While there are certainly other timing factors that could influence your success or the degree of your success, it's my belief that these four are the most critical.

You will need to recognize when the economic markets are ready for your product or service, when the technology is there to offer your product or service effectively and efficiently, when the political climate is friendly toward your industry, and when you're in the best place personally to make your business a success. Knowing when these key areas are aligned in the right way is a mark of a successful entrepreneur. If this seems like an impossible task, don't worry; very few first-generation entrepreneurs take the time to think about the timing of their businesses at all. While odds are that you'll be "wrong" about some aspect of the timing, the simple process of thinking about it puts you ahead of the curve and increases your chance of success.

To understand how critical alignment can be, consider the energy business. Energy efficiency was a hot topic in the 1970s, when gas prices were high due to the oil embargo and scientists were predicting that fossil fuels would be exhausted within 100 to 125 years. But solar power, wind power and other energy efficient businesses didn't take off back then. Why not? The answer lies in the technological advances of the time and in 1970s politics.

Forty years ago, it was difficult and expensive to harness the sun and the wind for power. Additionally, new advances in drilling technology continue to make building more reserves an easier and more affordable option. The political debate over how best to respond to scientists' predictions often focused on expanding U.S. control over resources—not on creating new eco-friendly, efficient technology. It just wasn't the right time for a business in energy efficiency. Today, it's obviously a different story.

It's likely that if you started an energy efficiency business in 2011, history will say you had "good timing." New technologies make wind power and solar power more efficient and exceptionally more affordable than 40 years ago. The political climate, too, was ready for a change. In particular, the 2010 BP Gulf oil spill led many people to call for more environmental protections and less drilling.

In 2011, the economic market was also perfect for starting a business in energy efficiency. Due to President Obama's push for energy independence and advances in "green" technology, small businesses can apply for grants and government funding for advances in energy efficiency and renewable energy technologies. They can do this through the Small Business Innovation Research program, the Small Business Technology Transfer program, and the Advance Research Projects Agency-Energy program.[34] Additionally, the U.S. government's 2009 stimulus package included $3.2 billion for state and local governments to use for projects that would reduce fossil fuel emissions, reduce total energy needs, improve energy efficiency and create new "green" jobs.[35] That's a lot of money available for businesses that didn't exist in the 1970s.

Although the Obama-era initiatives became less of a priority when President Trump came into office in 2017, the issue of energy is still paramount. Tesla, an electric-car manufacturing company that was founded in 2003, appears to be completely rewriting the book on fossil fuels in cars. They delivered 26,000 vehicles during the third quarter of 2017, and their Model S was one of the best selling all-electric cars in the United States in 2016.[36]

So, if you are in the mining business, your days as a business are probably numbered. But if you have an idea; if you're ready to invest a significant portion of your time and energy into a new company; and you have an interest in delivering energy more efficiently, effectively and cleaner; your timing is perfect. Energy efficiency is a hot topic that will likely remain a permanent trend.

Regardless of how perfectly-aligned the other three factors are, you have to be in the right place personally to start your business. If not, it can never be the perfect time. You won't have the energy, the focus, or the support to make it through the many struggles of launching a business.

Idea Inspiration

Ideas are power. What you envision, and where and how you get those ideas can also improve your chances for success. Many entrepreneurs birth their ideas almost by accident. They have a flash of insight and see a way to improve on a current product, service or business. Often, these ideas are inspired in the most counterintuitive places—such as in the shower or on the subway. Often, these thoughts occur on vacation. Think about it. The day-to-day stress of your life is not monopolizing your creative thinking and your brain is free to explore. So it does. This supports my point made earlier in Chapter Two about Integration. There are many benefits to scheduling time away from the office to think, to be creative and to relax.

Entrepreneurs see ideas in everything, and can find inspiration in the most mundane of activities. Take Jay Sorenson, the inventor of the coffee cup sleeve, as an example. Sorenson came up with the product in 1993, coinciding with a massive expansion of coffee shop chains and new boutique coffee shops. The idea was likely from an event as simple as receiving a paper cup of coffee that was too hot to hold.[37] Today, the coffee cup sleeve is everywhere. An intimate knowledge of what's available, *and* what's needed or could be done better often translates into a winning idea.

The "next big thing" could be as close as your random thoughts of "why doesn't **somebody** do *this*?" As a current example, have you thought about how hard it is to keep your iPad cover clean? The "this" is the better idea, and the "somebody" can be you—the first-generation entrepreneur!

Inspiration also strikes at work. According to a Wharton business professor, new ideas come from identifying inefficiency in the market, and then having an idea to correct that inefficiency.[38] That isn't surprising. Not only does previous work experience in the industry provide essential background knowledge in how the industry works, it also provides the best perspective on what *doesn't* work. Which industry you're in doesn't matter. Whether it's the service industry, manufacturing or telecommunications—as a former employee, you've seen firsthand how a product, service or process works from the inside out. You're the best person to know not only *what* could be done better, but *where* and *how* it could be done better. Paying attention to those everyday inspirations is part of what makes entrepreneurs who we are.

Idea success doesn't have to be accidental, either. Today, many good ideas come as a result of education, willpower and intense industry analysis. Colleges and universities around the country have recognized a need to provide education and guidance to students who are interested in starting their own business. According to the Ewing Marion Kauffman Foundation, the number of available courses for these aspiring entrepreneurs grew from 250 in 1985 to over 5,000 in 2008, and more than 400,000 students were taking them. The availability of degrees and specializations in entrepreneurship has seen a growing trend as well. In 1975, there were only about 100 formal majors, minors and certifications offered at colleges and universities, but in 2006, there were over 500. Recognizing the importance of these types of classes in the business curriculum, several schools began requiring that all students take classes in the principles of entrepreneurship in 2013.[39]

The Ohio State University in Columbus, Ohio, where my company is headquartered, is a good example of a school that provides education and support for students interested in pursuing entrepreneurship. OSU has an official academic center, the Keenan Center for Entrepreneurship housed in the Fisher College of Business.[40] This center strives to provide experiences, skills and resources to help students, professionals and community partners develop and apply an entrepreneurial mindset in the pursuit of their aspirations. The center began offering an entrepreneurship and innovation minor in 2015, which requires three core courses, one elective course and one practicum.

The minor provides students from multiple fields with a core understanding of how to develop a new start-up business, implement services or business models within an existing company, and create new products. Students will learn and use critical thinking skills as well as cross-disciplinary and problem-solving applications. The minor can be completed in 15 hours and five courses.[41]

In addition to formal education, aspiring entrepreneurs can also find free or low-cost help, support and resources through local Small Business Development Centers (SBDC). Dozens of host networks and hundreds of service delivery points throughout the U.S., District of Columbia, Guam, Puerto Rico, American Samoa and the US Virgin Islands offer assistance nearly anywhere.[42] The centers receive funding from a number of sources, including private individuals, colleges, universities, state governments, and the United States Small Business Administration. These educational programs provide aspiring entrepreneurs with the tools necessary to figure out both what the market needs at any given time and how to provide it—both of which are crucial to bringing good ideas to fruition.

Support Network

Getting a business off the ground is highly stressful. It can also be lonely. John C. Maxwell summarized it best: if you want to succeed as an entrepreneur, you have to have a solid support network, which can provide a sense of community as well as inspiration for new ways to approach common problems.[43]

There are many formal support networks throughout the country, groups such as the Entrepreneurs Organization (EO), Young Presidents Organization (YPO), Vistage and countless other resources. These support groups provide scaled tools for success and entrepreneurial development, including networking with other business leaders, private mentoring, workshops, and access to articles and information.

The Startup America Partnership is an independent, private-sector resource for entrepreneurs created in 2011 in partnership with the White House. The organization assists entrepreneurs through training and mentoring programs, and recruiting assistance. It also helps find scaled and reduced-cost critical services for new, cash-strapped business owners.[44] Many start-up businesses can access resources and find support at the local Chamber of Commerce, SCORE and the National Association of Small Businesses.

I am a member of EO, I have friends in YPO, and I also created my own networking support group called WANDA a few years ago with other business owners. The members of WANDA study each other's businesses, show tax returns, study data, and look for trends to determine who is growing their business most efficiently and having the most fun. We learn from each other's successes and challenges. The group has grown through the years and we now meet twice a year for once-in-a-lifetime events. WANDA is a great example of a successful group that was formed by its members—and we are not a chapter of a larger, national organization. We're a group of entrepreneurs with similar needs who band together to support each other and grow our businesses. The lesson here is that if you need something the current business environment doesn't provide, create it yourself.

In addition to traditional support groups, consider business solutions from companies such as Google, Amazon and Apple. Google supports small businesses through their integration of G

Suite tools such as email, calendar, Google documents and storage through Google Drive.[45] Using Google My Business,[46] your business appears in potential customers' search results for your business or businesses like yours. Google is a reliable, extremely affordable option for small businesses.

Similarly, Amazon supports their small business customers by giving them access to their business products, account management, payment solutions, and of course, their world-class fulfillment capabilities.[47] Apple offers iPhones, laptops, payment readers, sales tracking tools, and productivity apps and accessories.[48] So while you are considering the traditional support groups that can help you grow your business, also make sure your business aligns with powerhouse companies like Google, Amazon or Apple. It makes a huge difference in the amount of support you can receive.

Formal support networks and partners are critical for finding solutions to common problems and brainstorming what to do next. Formal support is essential, but not enough.

The most important sources of support for first-generation entrepreneurs are immediate family members and close friends. It is within these relationships that our enthusiasm for our businesses can be encouraged and nurtured—or squashed. It is critical that our most comfortable environment, our space with our friends and family, be "safe." As a first-generation entrepreneur, there will be many times when you will be temporarily depressed, confused, angry, or ridiculously euphoric, and you need your family and closest friends to unconditionally support you during these periods.

> The most important sources of support for first-generation entrepreneurs are immediate family members and close friends.

You must also remember that most people do not have the courage or gumption to be a first-generation entrepreneur. These are the "naysayers." Those who don't have that courage will often criticize your risk taking and efforts to succeed because your actions make them realize their own limitations and shortcomings.

At a conscious or subconscious level, they do not want you to succeed, and their advice to you is often given with a perhaps subconscious desire for you to fail. Be very, very careful with any advice you receive from others who have not attempted (success-fully or unsuccessfully) their own ventures. And, make sure to take solace in the relationships with those who champion you.

It is within these close, supportive relationships that you will find the strength to overcome failures and progress through the five stages of business success as I've coined them:

- Intoxicating Stage

- Trapped Stage

- Light at the End of the Tunnel Stage

- Acceleration Stage, and

- Sustainable Stage

Let's talk about how to integrate through them all.

5
STAGE ONE—THE
INTOXICATING STAGE

THE FIRST OF the five stages of success first-generation entrepreneurs go through is called the *Intoxicating Stage*. This stage is
full of excitement and raw enthusiasm. Entrepreneurs experience
a tremendous sense of freedom and independence when they
realize the business is real, it's theirs and they're on their own.
This is compelling, particularly if they've worked for someone
else in some way.

Although the Intoxicating Stage is positive and exhilarating,
it's also all consuming. Entrepreneurs put in 80-hour weeks and
make sacrifices because they're so smitten and intoxicated with
being independent. At this point, they don't mind the extra hours.
They are motivated. They can't get enough of it because they know
they will live and die by their own efforts. Even their support
system—their family, friends and professional contacts—gives
them a "pass" for keeping crazy hours, spending their evenings
and weekends at the office, and talking endlessly about their new

business. They are living on adrenaline because they know that if they succeed, this new venture will translate to independence, freedom and flexibility for the rest of their lives.

Entrepreneurs at this stage are probably not doing much integrating, but depending on where they are in their life with family and kids, planned experience sharing is more important now than ever. They must be very deliberate in prioritizing the people in their lives.

Most first-generation entrepreneurs at this stage are also extremely naïve about what it takes to succeed. They are doing everything alone, and they're not quite sure what comes next, or even who to talk to about it.

The unfortunate reality is that most entrepreneurs never make it out of this stage. Some will wear themselves out with their myriad duties—winning clients, making sales, managing inventories, negotiating with suppliers, hiring employees, implementing processes and systems, ensuring timely deliveries, managing cash flow and networking. They never find the energy to expand their businesses into more than a one-person shop. Others will simply be unable to gather enough clients, sell enough products, develop the proper processes and systems, or raise enough money to pay the bills.

For those entrepreneurs who simply want to be their own boss and do what they love, making ends meet in this stage may be all the success they need. If they want to expand into something bigger though, they will have to make it out of their Intoxication Stage. To do that, they will need support of their family and business network. They'll need to stay confident in their own ideas while they consider the input of others.

When you're in the Intoxicating Stage, it may be too early in your business career to join a formal organization such as EO or Vistage, but it is still important to develop a support network of other entrepreneurs. You

> It's very important to surround yourself with people who have "been there done that," and who can share their experiences with you.

can search your local area for organizations or Meetup groups that support start-ups or young professionals—and you may need to form one yourself, as I did with WANDA. It's very important to surround yourself with people who have "been there done that," and who can share their experiences with you. You may not be ready to take on an advisory board at this stage, but finding those people who can support and mentor you is invaluable. Seeking out this type of support is not something most entrepreneurs think about in the Intoxicating Stage. But it is an insightful, unique and unusual perspective—and it's critical to your success and happiness.

Dealing with Naysayers

First-generation entrepreneurs sometimes find it difficult to stay confident in their business ideas once they've begun really putting themselves and their ideas out into the market. Even though they started their business for a reason—and with a great idea of how to do something better, different, or new—they may begin to doubt themselves and their ideas as they get input from other people.

Input is important and you should take note of every piece you're given, but at this point, in order to move forward in your business, it's critical that you keep your confidence level high. Surround yourself with the friends, family and other first-generation entrepreneurs who do support you and believe in what you're doing. Catalogue the input you receive from others, but don't act on it yet.

As mentioned earlier, you'll often be faced with "naysayers" in the early stages of business. These people generally don't have the personal fortitude to be entrepreneurs themselves, but measure their own worth against others. It is the naysayer's natural tendency to discount everyone else's ideas and to knock other people down. In order to make it to Stage Two, it is vitally important that you do not let these people influence you. Don't allow them to make you doubt yourself. If you can receive feedback and input—even from people who don't agree with or see the value in what you're doing—and still continue to hold fast to your ideas and your plan, you will eventually make it into the next stage of success.

Some of the most influential business owners, innovators, entertainers and authors have faced their share of naysayers and have succeeded despite them.

The band U2 is, in my opinion, one of the biggest and best bands of all time. They've won 22 Grammys, had 31 songs on the Billboard Top 100 list, and sold over 150 million records. When the group first started out, they faced a steady stream of rejections, most of which are now displayed in the Rock and Roll Hall of Fame in Cleveland. The band's first manager, Paul McGuinness, said "I was amazed at the quality and talent and ambition of these four musicians, yet we couldn't get a record deal. Everyone in the world passed on U2 before we finally found a home at Island Records."[49]

In 1957, an aspiring author named Harper Lee delivered her first manuscript to the publisher and it was quickly rejected. Over the next two years, what would eventually become "To Kill a Mockingbird" was completely rewritten several times before it was finally published in 1960. The book was at the top of the bestseller list for over 40 weeks, was awarded the Pulitzer Prize in 1961, and sold more than 40 million copies over the course of five decades. Lee told Writer's Digest, "I would advise anyone who aspires to a writing career that before developing his talent he would be wise to develop a thick hide."[50]

In the music and book industries, naysayers such as a producer or publisher who say "No" will stop you in your tracks and send you back to the drawing board. Naysayers in the business world can be hiding in your support network, and don't always hit you with a strong, obvious rejection. They can be that doubting voice among the positive, encouraging feedback you receive from others—the voice that wears you down over time. Sometimes their negative influence is subtle, but it can be just as damaging to your confidence as an emphatic rejection.

Consider this example.

You and your college roommate both graduated and found jobs. She found one as a marketing professional in the healthcare industry; you started as a video editor for a large local advertising agency. Your roommate asked you to join a newly emerging young professionals' networking group that had eight members with steady, promising jobs in the marketing and advertising fields. It was a great fit for you both. The group included fresh, mostly-optimistic people that you liked on a personal level. One of its members was Mike, a cautious, glass-half-empty and slightly negative kind of guy. You didn't recognize him as a naysayer at first, because you were young, excited, and just there to network and have fun.

Three years later, still employed at the advertising agency, you stumble upon and create the exact technology needed to solve a video-editing problem your entire industry needed to move to the next level. And the beauty was, no one else had thought of it.

Bursting with excitement, you decide to quit your job at the agency and start your own business. For six months, you're living the dream and experiencing the Intoxicating Stage—working hard, making sales and riding a creative high. Things couldn't seem brighter.

Almost.

You've still been going faithfully to your young professionals' networking group, and have gained valuable marketing and advertising advice. The problem is Mike. You've come to confide in your group of peers, but Mike has rained on your parade since the first day you mentioned your business venture idea. Mike is a marketing wizard and gives a lot to the group, but he's not an entrepreneur. He's told you your idea has probably already been thought of, you'll have to grovel for a job when your business collapses and he constantly quotes statistics about failed startups.

You're pretty much done with Mike's point of view, but you keep going to meetings because you value the other members, and you feel a loyalty to them and your college roommate, who is also still a member and good friend. On the way to the last few meetings, you've felt conflicted and stressed, and your participation and engagement has dwindled considerably.

It's obviously time for you to find a new group—one made up of entrepreneurs like you. Or form your own. If you spend your precious time with a group that's going to help you go where you want to be, you're integrating. If you internalize the things you learned—even Mike's statistics on failed startups, which can only drive you to not be among them—you're integrating. Your friends from the old group will still be your friends. And Mike will still be Mike.

It's amazing but wholly true—even ONE naysayer like Mike can detract from your excitement about your new business and have a negative impact on your drive, focus and business success. And that naysayer can be someone you're very tied to emotionally—like your dad, your brother, or your best friend.

Today, my mom is one of my biggest cheerleaders. When I first started my business, she was my loving, unintentional naysayer. I say it like that because I know now that she was coming from a place of concern and had a lack of understanding. At the time I didn't see it that way. I had grown up with the expectation that I was going to go to college and get a great job. The perception of my being an executive with a big company was really important to my mom.

I'll never forget the day I told her I wasn't going to interview for a job, and that I was going to start a business instead. She cried. It was such a horrible thing for me to hear how disappointed she was. I was so crushed, and felt like I let her down, but I knew I was not cut out for corporate America. Even at age 22, I knew that was not going to be me.

My mom is extremely risk-averse, and couldn't understand why I would ever want to start my own business, let alone work as a financial planner. She didn't have anything to compare it to, so it was foreign to her.

Despite her doubts and the criticism of my brothers, I moved forward with my dream to start my own business. And as many entrepreneurs experience at the beginning of their journey, I failed mathematically and economically the first few years and was barely scraping by. But by year five, things started to gel and my business was taking off.

Today, everything has completely shifted. Although she may never fully understand what I do or the obstacles I've overcome since launching my business, I have my mom's full support. I may not be the CEO of a big company she had originally dreamed I'd be, but I am the CEO of my own company. I have followed my heart, and am successful, happy and fulfilled. And isn't that what all parents want for their children?

It's a challenge when your naysayers are people closest to you. They love you and they want to help you, but often they don't understand and don't know how to support you. Their concern turns them into your loving, unintentional naysayers.

Whether your naysayers are your career decision makers, members of a networking group, or part of your family, you can't listen to what they say. You need to do what U2, Harper Lee and every other successful person who has been doubted and rejected does: forge ahead. Surround yourself with people who are positive, supportive and realistic. When I meet someone who is starting a business, I am optimistic and sincere in my excitement for that person. In addition to that, I try to give those individuals a heads up about the challenges they will soon face, like being vulnerable to their first employee, or confusing hope with a strategy.

Too few people have the gumption to be an entrepreneur. But we're out there, and if you are reading this book, you are one of us, too. The journey is difficult, and those who have the courage to pursue their dream, launch their business and become intoxicated by it, will eventually transition to the second phase of business success: the Trapped Stage.

6
STAGE TWO—THE TRAPPED STAGE

AS FIRST-GENERATION ENTREPRENEURS go through the five stages of success, they experience the excitement and exhilaration of the Intoxicating Stage on one end of the spectrum. But what's to follow on the opposite end of the spectrum is not so exciting and much less exhilarating.

In the second stage, which I call the *Trapped Stage*, entrepreneurs begin to see how hard success can be. Their business earns revenue at a predictable and reliable enough rate that it is solvent for the immediate, foreseeable future. They've hired staff to address the mundane, yet important, administrative tasks associated with keeping a business running. They are "all in" from an emotional, intellectual, and financial perspective, but the enthusiasm from Stage One is fading.

The reality sets in as they begin to live with the decisions they make in order to follow their dreams. In some instances, entrepreneurs left a stable, well-paying job with a guaranteed income and now their future income is uncertain. They made financial commitments, such as buying equipment or signing leases, and know they need to make more of those types of purchases and agreements in order to move forward, but the financial risk is high. They may have hired employees—hard working individuals with families and commitments of their own who have also left safe, stable jobs to come work for the new entrepreneur.

To top it off, most entrepreneurs tell so many people about their new business that it would be humiliating or embarrassing to back out. They don't want to abandon their plans and aspirations, or let their families down. And the last thing on earth they want to do is to admit their naysayers were right, and listen to those same people say, "I told you so."

The Trapped Stage feels like it happened overnight and came from every angle imaginable. It's emotional, financial, personal and completely overwhelming. Failure at this point not only affects the entrepreneur, but the lives of others as well. And for many of these entrepreneurs, they are no longer in control. Instead, their survival is in the hands of someone or something else—customers, lessors, the bank or the market.

The Trapped Stage is not for the faint of heart. Everything is on the line and the entrepreneur has to execute or be out of business, all while putting on a brave face. If the entrepreneur can put on that brave face, his or her employees will never be the wiser to the pressures of the Trapped Stage. Knowing that these employees need to remain engaged and excited, the entrepreneur must go directly from the Intoxicating Stage to the Light at the End of the Tunnel Stage, but doing so only adds to the his or her pressure.

> The Trapped Stage is not for the faint of heart. Everything is on the line and the entrepreneur has to execute or be out of business, all while putting on a brave face.

Call it what you want—do or die, win or lose, all or nothing. There are no gray areas. It's a very difficult place to be, and entrepreneurs must fight to get through it. They have no other choice but to press on.

A friend and client of mine was a well-paid employee of a large Fortune 500 company for many years. He made over a million dollars a year, but was on the road all the time, away from his family, and he had grown tired of the drill. He'd always wanted to own his own business but had not been able to make a move— partly out of fear, partly because the timing wasn't quite right.

After a few years of hard work and networking, he identified a company in his industry he could buy. It was a perfect situation where the owner was ready to sell and the employees were willing to stay and work for a new owner. My friend sought advice from a mentor, consulted with the advisors at Gerber and hired a lawyer to put together a letter of intent. He was in the Intoxicating Stage, where everything was exciting, hopeful and exhilarating. However, the Trapped Stage was looming just around the corner. Once the purchase was official, that financial investment and commitment to the employees who trusted in him was made. He had shared his dream and ambition with his network of family, friends and nearly everyone else who knew him. To back out at that point would have not only been expensive, but he also would have let down his employees and all others who believed in him. Just like that, things got real, and he moved from the Intoxicating Stage to the Trapped Stage as his feelings of excitement and intoxication were replaced by uncertainty and pressure.

You have to prepare yourself emotionally when moving from the Intoxicating Stage to the Trapped Stage because it happens so fast. Part of being an entrepreneur is managing the big swings between your positive and negative energy that result from shifts like this. And keeping those around you in the loop with deliberate, day-to-day communications will help prepare everyone for the changes that will come.

The Trapped Stage doesn't always happen in a vacuum. Another colleague of mine experienced this stage while dealing with unexpected outside factors. She owned a business that was cash flow neutral, and could see a demand for more business was coming. She considered signing a lease to accommodate the growth that was anticipated, and recruited the employees she would need if things went as planned. However, she felt very trapped knowing she had to make a big commitment financially and to her potential employees if the business was going to succeed. Adding to the stress in the midst of her Trapped State was that her husband was also an entrepreneur whose business had an unexpected capital shortage and was taking a financial hit. They didn't have excess capital available to support the growth of her business and the negative bump in his at the same time. Opportunity cost was part of her challenge, but with the curveball hitting her husband's business, she was really in a bad position. It took a toll on both her and the family, and they had to cut every expense from their life that was not financially essential. It also suspended their business goals for at least another year or two.

The Trapped Stage happens to big, once successful businesses as well. Skybus, established in 2007, was based in Columbus, Ohio at what is now known as the John Glenn International Airport. It created 450 jobs, offered direct flights to cities all over the country, and had the most inexpensive fares in the industry. Not to mention it was a huge source of pride to many local investors, state development officials and prominent companies such as Nationwide Insurance, Huntington Bank and Battelle, the nation's leading research institute. Its success was short lived, as mismanagement resulted in lousy food, late planes and customers stranded on Christmas due to mechanical mishaps. Additionally, the price of oil was increasing, bookings were down, and the economy was tanking. The nail in the coffin was when First Data Corp, Skybus's credit card processor, would not allow the airline to include credit card orders on its balance sheet until the flights occurred. Feeling trapped, Skybus's executive team and board members launched a desperate quest to raise 30 to 70 million dollars in the final hours to try and save the company. They came up short. Skybus was forced to declare bankruptcy after just 10 months, resulting in passengers stranded all over the country, employee layoffs and dozens of creditors stuck with unpaid bills.[51]

The demise of Skybus taught us how delicate a new business can be no matter how successful it may seem in the beginning.

Another example is Sidecar, a ride-sharing app launched in 2012 that had a leg up on Uber in terms of technology and innovation. It offered features that were ahead of its time, but the company spent more time upgrading the product than marketing to their customers. On the other hand, Uber had an efficient sales and marketing team that secured wider brand visibility and expanded their service area. Sidecar couldn't make it out of the Trapped Stage and went out of business in 2015. General Motors acquired their assets.[52]

The Trapped Stage is a double whammy because in addition to financial pressures, it causes high levels of stress, contributes to poor health, and places significant strains on relationships with friends and family. Many entrepreneurs gain weight, and develop anxiety or depression. They neglect their health by not getting enough sleep, failing to exercise and not eating right.[53] The Trapped Stage can be lonely, too. Not only are you feeling trapped during this stage, but your support system may not be available to help you because of other life circumstances. There may be personal situations such as a sick child, a dying parent, or a child going off to college that prevent even the most supportive spouse from understanding and being available to help you. These intense and delicate situations make the Trapped Stage even harder for the entrepreneur.

The first time I experienced the Trapped Stage, I was young and newly married. Emily and I had just purchased our first house and were expecting our first child. I didn't want to take away what should be one of the happiest times of her life by sharing the burden I was carrying in the Trapped Stage.

There's an upside for all entrepreneurs in this stage. This is when success comes through sheer will, personal strength, and very deliberate decisions and strategies. If you have a good support network of advisors around you, often sheer brute force can get you through the Trapped Stage. It doesn't have to be all luck. It won't be pretty or easy, but if you stay focused, you will get through it.

To help you force your way through the Trapped Stage, revisit the plans and decisions you made when you first started your business. Review your marketing plan, address your core values, and take solace in the strength of decisions your business was built on. When your foundation is strong, you will gain the confidence to push through the rough and stressful times.

You will have to make many important decisions when you are in the Trapped Stage, and you must understand the risks associated with every decision. That includes financial risks, employee risks, and business risks. Set a limit on how much of your own money you're prepared to invest into your business. Try to avoid matters like signing a lease personally if you can, although that is not always possible. If you have to invest your own personal money in the business, do so in a way that does not do irreparable harm to your personal balance sheet. You may want to consult a professional to make sure you are buying what you need the "right" way from an accounting perspective. Be careful about accepting money from friends or family that they aren't willing to lose.

Meet with a lawyer or business-consulting firm (like Gerber) that understands high growth businesses. They can advise on how to structure your business and manage staff to minimize stress. You may also benefit from talking with a business coach or therapist to help manage your many priorities so you don't end up at the bottom of your own priority list, or worse, not on the list at all.

When entrepreneurs are stressed, one of the first things to go is exercise, when really it should remain one of the highest priorities. Lack of time, mental fatigue and physical exhaustion are easy and convenient excuses for not working out. You may feel it's selfish to take the time to do something for yourself when many other people's lives are dependent upon your business's success or demise. Exercise actually helps entrepreneurs with business. It stimulates the release of hormones that boosts mood, jumpstarts energy and increases stamina. It also lowers stress hormones like cortisol and adrenaline that help you feel focused, calm and relaxed.[54] I advise you to schedule exercise several times each week, early in the morning if possible. If conflicts arise, reschedule that client meeting and protect your exercise time. Exercise will make you feel better about all the roles you have in your life, whether it be spouse, parent, friend, or business owner.

Here's a healthy dose of tough love: Getting through the Trapped Stage is a rite of passage. It's part of the deal, and as stressful and impossible as it may seem at the time, you need to stick with it, put in the effort, and get through it. You'll save the business, and you'll learn what you are made of. When you have the personal fortitude to survive and make it through the misgivings, the doubts and the instability, you will enter the Light at the End of the Tunnel Stage.

7
STAGE THREE—THE LIGHT AT THE END OF THE TUNNEL STAGE

AFTER ENDURING THE stress, pressure and desperation of the Trapped Stage, things start to finally come together as entrepreneurs enter Stage Three, the *Light at the End of the Tunnel Stage.* This stage usually occurs between years three and five when the business is finally on level ground, finances pick up, customers sign on, and long-term contracts are collected. Entrepreneurs begin to see enough demand for their supply, products and services, and they start to feel confident they aren't going out of business tomorrow. Cash flow is reliable, and they are more comfortable with making longer-term bets such as hiring higher-wage staff or contractors, buying more equipment and expanding facilities.

For many entrepreneurs, the Light at the End of the Tunnel Stage is a big sense of relief. The constant state of fear and anxiety over expenses and finances are alleviated, and they feel like they can begin to have fun again. These entrepreneurs start to remember why they started their business, and the enthusiasm returns. In the back of their minds, though, a sense of caution still exists somewhat because they know they are still treading on delicate ground.

For example, entrepreneurs in this stage often have to hire people to support the growth they anticipate before they can actually afford to. They faced this challenge in the Trapped Stage also, but their business is now more stable. The new hires help with the additional workload, and also improve the working environment so the entrepreneur can go out and sell. Since job satisfaction of the business's current employees hinges on being surrounded by strong, capable coworkers, it's important that entrepreneurs are recruiting experienced, solid, A+ players to the team. The entrepreneur walks a thin line, but knows adding quality new hires is necessary for the business to move forward. It's possible that an entrepreneur's revenue will grow in the Light at the End of the Tunnel Stage, but their profit and cash will most likely not.

I've always believed and have told my clients that entrepreneurs in general are only three bad decisions away from being homeless. Entrepreneurs in the Light at the End of the Tunnel Stage may be only *one* bad decision away from being homeless. Homelessness may be a slight exaggeration, but the point is true. In a business's early years, short-term, temporary failures— failures that could be overcome if the business was a little more secure—often lead to total, permanent failure. Unfortunately, many entrepreneurs who suffer short-term, temporary failures in their beginning stages can't overcome them. The loss of a key client or key employee undercuts the business's tenuous financial solvency or the barely established flow of daily operations. They may

> I've always believed and have told my clients that entrepreneurs in general are only three bad decisions away from being homeless.

experience difficulties with finances, key relationships, burn out, and/or lack of personal time. Businesses at this point don't have the bandwidth to survive a negative turn of events, and the entrepreneur once again scrambles to make ends meet. Some entrepreneurs may have a lingering anxiety and fear of tumbling back into the Trapped Stage or going out of business altogether. The slightest problem or an element of bad luck could cause everything to fall apart.

Back in 2005, I invested a substantial amount of money, time and relationships in a side business that sold high-end, gently used items for people who didn't want the hassle of selling those items themselves. We set up "drop spots" around the city where our customers could conveniently drop off their items. We handled the whole transaction, kept our customers informed, and charged a 20 percent commission. We even started a program with one of the largest independent jewelry stores in the country where we sold jewelry bought from their customers in exchange for store credit. Golf clubs, watches and high-end small items that could be easily shipped worked perfectly for our business. We had successfully made it through the Intoxication and Trapped Stages, and were enjoying the relief and comfort of the Light at the End of the Tunnel Stage. We had rapidly-growing revenues, we were building out the infrastructure, and sales were really starting to take off. Then the financial crisis of 2008 hit. Most economists say this was the worst economic disaster since the Great Depression of 1929, and it occurred despite the efforts of the Federal Reserve and the Treasury Department.[55] The capital markets dried up, and I needed to focus my attention on making sure my own business, Gerber LLC, endured the crisis. Unfortunately, the side-business ended up going under because of a combination of financial pressures, market pressures and people pressures. We didn't make any bad decisions that caused it to fail, but the business was still in its infancy when the economy tanked. It was bad luck—and a perfect example of just how fragile a new business is, even in Stage Three—and how something out of the entrepreneur's control can cause it to fail.

Keys to Success

If your business manages to sidestep bad luck, overcomes its temporary setbacks and makes it to the Light at the End of the Tunnel Stage, you will need a solid strategy for growth. There are four keys strategies that will help you get there.

- The first key strategy to getting through the Light at the End of the Tunnel Stage is learning to work "on" your business rather than "in" your business. This is the stage where your time becomes a crucial commodity, and your energy and focus are critical. Because you are focused on "big picture" projects, you must delegate the day-to-day responsibilities to another leader. It can be a difficult transition to make, because in the first two stages you were the leader not only in spirit but also in form. As the business grows, it becomes impossible to be the leader in form. You will be less available and must rely on the leadership team to carry out the daily operations of the business. It's very important that you embrace that and not run from it. I hear stories all the time about entrepreneurs who swoop in like a hurricane after weeks of being away and change everything. It's a huge disruption to the business. You must recognize and accept that the business will go on without you. You need to delegate someone to handle the operations and administrative side of things, such as opening and closing, taking emergency phone calls, and dealing with upset customers. This frees you to work "on" the business and lead it forward.

- The second key to success in Stage Three centers on obtaining strategic advice from consultants, mentors or an advisory board. Knowing what you don't know is a crucial component to success, as is the knowledge that there are things *you don't even know* you don't know. There may be problems you can't see or upcoming challenges you would not have seen until it's too late. If you recruit the right

mentors or people to your advisory board, specifically entrepreneurs who have had success, they can help you. They
will give you a different perspective, quick solutions, and
confidence in what to do or what not to do. Some of the
decisions you are faced with seem huge and monumental
but really aren't, and the perspective of your mentors or
advisory board will help you to not make mountains out
of molehills. An advisory board or consulting team can
assist you in viewing your business and your business's
goals through perspectives and backgrounds other than
your own.

- Implementing a management system is the third key to
success in the Light at the End of Tunnel Stage. As we
discussed in Chapter Three, systems such as EOS, MAP
Management Consulting and Rockefeller Habits help
new entrepreneurs avoid mistakes, or at least minimize
the impact of them. A challenge most entrepreneurs have
is they don't know about these systems early enough, and
once they do, they often can't afford to hire someone to
help implement the systems. It's possible to self-implement,
but it can be difficult to fully master the process, educate
your leadership team, hold everyone accountable and stay
on top of your business responsibilities all at the same
time. Even though I was enlightened and aware about
EOS and had a solid understanding of it, I still needed
an implementer to help me get the system established at
Gerber. The implementer helped me identify my business's
core values, develop communication rhythms and frame
the right decisions. Whether you self-implement or hire
an implementer, having a management system in place
helps ensure you'll make fewer mistakes and improves the
odds of your success.

- An integrated work life and planned experience sharing,
previously discussed in Chapters Two and Three are the
fourth keys to success in the Light at the End of the Tunnel

Stage. This is where you establish good work/life habits, something that most entrepreneurs are not successful at during the first two stages. Now you have money to solve problems and more time to do it, so you no longer need to brute force your way through solutions. You need to seek enjoyment, and engage in and be present for those things that are important to you outside of work. If your personal goals are to get married and have a family, you want to try to be home for dinner, even if you have to go back to work later in the evening. Make it to your kids' sporting events, try to exercise at least three times per week, and give yourself the freedom to spend one 24-hour period per month where you don't think about work at all.

Although this stage has its own stress and pressures, it is entirely possible to get through it quickly and realize sustainability and stability. Any company that has been in business 10 years or more has gone through this stage, and comes out stronger and more successful.

One such company is a client of ours, The Spot Athletics, headquartered here in Columbus, Ohio. The Spot Athletics is a private training facility that makes world class coaching, education and training methods available to anyone in the community, from families and senior citizens to young athletes and professional athletes.[56] Its founder and Head Strength Coach, JL Holdsworth, knew he needed to open seven locations to reach his goals before he retired. We helped him plan, based on how long it would take to open a location and for it to be profitable, as well as gave him a new strategy for compensating his coaches that helped recruit the best talent in the industry. He experienced the Trapped Stage as he was signing new leases and hiring new coaches, but entered into the Light at the End of the Tunnel stage as he successfully added enough new clients every month to offset the expense. He had a very clear plan and it is working. He has blown right through Stage Three, and continues to grow his business the way he always wanted.

Success stories like this are all around you. They serve as motivation and inspiration when you are going through the ups and downs of each stage. After you have delegated your day-to-day responsibilities, formed an advisory board, implemented a management system, and set good integration habits, your business will start to be more stable. You will then move forward into Stage Four: the Acceleration Stage.

8
STAGE FOUR—THE ACCELERATION STAGE

AS A BUSINESS transitions from the Light at the End of the Tunnel Stage to Stage Four, the *Acceleration Stage*, the groundwork has already been laid for significant progress. While growth may not be evident in all parts of the business all at the same time, there should be measured improvements in the financial, marketing and process side of the business, with a good chance of the business being profitable. The business either has become or has the opportunity to be a significant player in the space it defines.

This has happened thanks to lessons learned in the previous stages. By the time entrepreneurs reach Stage Four, they have identified how to scale their business profitably and healthfully. There is enough momentum in the business for entrepreneurs to plan to make investments in people, equipment, capital expenses, time and processes to grow the business more rapidly. Their relationship with the business has improved and it is clearly moving forward.

Entrepreneurs in this stage begin to build their leadership teams, expand their benefits program and develop robust employee-employer relationships. In the early stages of a business, there often aren't formal policies and procedures in place to address employee situations such as paid time off, flextime and work from home policies. Therefore, most entrepreneurs handle these matters on a case-by-case basis and on a personal level. As the business grows, this can lead to inconsistent situations from person-to-person and from year-to-year. Formal policies and procedures quickly become necessary to ensure all situations are handled the same way for everyone. Most entrepreneurs may not think to implement formal policies and procedures for situations that haven't happened yet, but they should consider developing them in the early stages of the business to avoid future conflicts.

Entrepreneurs in the Acceleration Stage are continuing to master stress management, integration and not letting the pressures of the business derail them personally. They are getting better at sustaining positive energy, and keeping their spouses and families happy. While short-term temporary failures can and often do still occur at this stage, they are unlikely to destabilize the business in the same way as in the beginning stages. By this point, the business is stable enough that few problems can really shake it.

Also in this stage is when entrepreneurs begin the transition from employee owner to investor owner. This transition begins in the Light of the End of the Tunnel Stage, but entrepreneurs are still working "in" the business—doing whatever it takes to keep the business going, such as opening and closing the store, answering phones, and performing the day-to-day responsibilities because it needs to be done and someone needs to do it. A very small amount of time is spent as an investor owner, working "on" the business. As the business transitions into the Acceleration Stage, entrepreneurs need to take on the role of investor owner and spend more of their time problem solving, writing business plans, and hiring managers to take over sales and operations, for example. They often can't emotionally shed the employee owner responsibilities. Entrepreneurs typically struggle with this transition during the Acceleration Stage—they know what needs to be done, but the employee owner and investor owner roles are fighting each other. Entrepreneurs continue to work on this transition as they grow through the Acceleration Stage.

The growth experienced in the Acceleration Stage is the financial cornerstone that allows the business to assume more risk and be insulated from mistakes. Risks don't go away as the business moves forward.

> Risks don't go away as the business moves forward. Entrepreneurs in this stage are just more aware of the risks and have a better understanding of the ones that matter.

Entrepreneurs in this stage are just more aware of the risks and have a better understanding of the ones that matter. They are better equipped to manage those risks, tackle them more willingly, and even view them as an opportunity to improve and get ahead of the competition.

The timing couldn't be more perfect, because in order to move to Stage Five, innovation must be the fabric of a business's culture. Innovation, in and of itself, is both a risk and an opportunity. It's crucial that entrepreneurs embrace change, double or triple down on innovation and grow. This means creating more effective processes, implementing new ideas and improving existing services in order to be a sustainable, long-term business. It can be disruptive and uncomfortable to take a chance on the unknown, but without goals for growth and room for expansion, a business will become stifled.

Many people have accused Amazon of being a small business killer and if you own a sporting goods distribution business in a small town, you would probably agree. A typical small business that competes with Amazon is going to lose. My advice to you is this: don't compete with them. What you need to do instead is innovate.

Make a spectacular product—something that is unique, adds value and is like nothing else out there—and use Amazon to distribute and market it for you. Partner with technologies such as Alexa to fulfill your orders. Don't take on the giants. Innovate —and figure out how to use them to grow your business.

One example of someone who did exactly that is Robert Wang of Ontario, inventor of the Instant Pot. The Instant Pot combines common cooking functions such as pressure-cooking, slow cooking and sautéing in a single appliance. Robert developed it after realizing his busy schedule prevented him from preparing a healthy meal for his family. So he recruited two engineers, invested $350,000 of his own money and in 18 months, the Instant Pot was developed. And while Robert deserves much of the credit for Instant Pot's success, he's the first to acknowledge that he couldn't have done it without Amazon. In 2010, after experiencing declining sales in Ontario, Robert took advantage of Amazon's shipping program, Fulfillment by Amazon. As a result, Instant Pot's sales have doubled every year since 2011, and during Black Friday 2017, it was in the top five items sold by Amazon and Target, and in the top three items sold at Kohl's. He's done it as a homegrown hardware business with 50 employees, and no venture capital funding, while spending almost nothing on advertising. Amazon turned Instant Pot into a major empire almost overnight.[57] Robert innovated, and used Amazon to make his business a success.

My friend Sonny Balani has embraced innovation for years. His father, Peter, started Balani Custom Clothes in 1961. What began as a small business in Chicago has now grown to 14 locations, and they continue to offer handcrafted suits, taking pride in the finest detail and focusing on superior customer service.[58] Sonny accompanied me on a visit to Amazon in 2017, where we learned about a new technology that could potentially give a consumer the ability to order custom clothes based on scanned measurements, and feedback about fit, color and comfort. While this technology might be perceived to be a threat to Sonny's business, it's not; it actually presents an opportunity for him.

Someone will need to make these custom items that the technology designs, and my bet is on Sonny. Balani Custom Clothes has been in business for over 56 years and it's because they've never stopped innovating.

Walmart is another example of a large company that continues to embrace change, innovate and grow. Walmart's Founder, Sam Walton, made sure the company's always been two steps ahead of what people want for over 50 years. He was known for saying, "To succeed in this world, you have to change all of the time."[59] And he practiced what he preached. He was the first to use universal bar codes, which added ease and accuracy to the checkout process. He pioneered the Walmart Supercenter concept, which combines a one-stop shopping experience for groceries and general merchandise. The company introduced online shopping in 2000, site-to-store ordering in 2007, and online grocery pickup in 2016.

On the flip side, we've all heard about companies that failed to innovate and went out of business. Toys "R" Us filed for bankruptcy in September of 2017 because it was billions of dollars in debt —a debt incurred long before Amazon entered the picture. The company couldn't afford to stay competitive, pay their employees or make their stores a nice place to shop. Instead of innovating by adding playrooms where children could play with toys or providing a party space for birthdays, Toys "R" Us spent $400 million a year just to service their debt.[60]

Another company that failed to innovate was Kodak. Kodak filed for bankruptcy protection in 2012 after the capturing of a "Kodak moment" was replaced by digital cameras, sharing photos online and smart phones that included a high-quality camera. Kodak saw these changes coming and even tried to embrace them by investing in the necessary technology and creating its own digital camera, but Kodak failed to understand that "online photo sharing was a new business, not a way to expand the printing business."[61]

It doesn't matter how well known a business is or how successful it's become. Entrepreneurs in the Acceleration Stage shouldn't get too comfortable. They must learn to adapt, innovate and reinvent themselves to survive.

While innovation is crucial in this stage, it's also important not to let it consume all of your time. It can be difficult for entrepreneurs to scale either their businesses or their work/life relationships in a manner that works for them. To live within the Acceleration Stage, you have to learn to integrate more than ever to maintain relationships with your spouse, your family and your friends. I advise our clients to be very specific in how they want to live life deliberately and to separate their life goals into four categories: what they want for themselves, their families, their business and their friends. These categories may vary according to the individual, but I encourage you to envision where you want to be in each of your own categories in 20 to 25 years. Then ask yourself, "What needs to happen in 10 years to get to where I want to be in 20 to 25 years? What needs to happen next year to meet my 10-year goal? What needs to happen in the next 90 days to be where I need to be a year from now?" When you plan in reverse, it forces you to consider only what is most important. The Acceleration Stage is the first big opportunity you will have to look at what you're doing and carve out the things that aren't productive, aren't getting you to your planned goal or are a waste of your time. One thing I've become very good at is spending time on things that are core to my personal or business mission. I've become very focused and priority minded, and the Acceleration Stage has given me the freedom to do that.

The Acceleration Stage is often the time when entrepreneurs really need to consider bringing in professional management. Professional managers are experienced managers from outside your own company who have proven abilities in managing operations or subject expertise. They aren't necessarily entrepreneurs, but they have a lot of experience and know how to grow a business. I've seen companies make huge strides when utilizing professional managers and it can be so much more effective than trying to do everything yourself.

I've watched businesses that have been built organically—meaning they promote from within and don't bring in anyone new from the outside—grow modestly. This modest growth can't compare to the company that supplements their core team with at least one professional manager. When you look at the financial performances of those companies that do and those that don't, there is a night and day difference.

We see the differences among our own clients. One of our clients hired a high-ranking operations professional from a large company to be his professional manager and oversee his operations. His business has taken off. Another client has grown his business through his own personal sales efforts, and while he's had some success and his business has definitely improved, this business is not as profitable as the client who hired a professional manager.

While hiring a professional manager is an important next step, you should understand that this transition is not easy. Adding professional management can be a painful process for your current employees because it disrupts the cultural history and DNA of the company. A professional manager identifies inefficient habits that may have been adopted as your business grew. While you may have hired the best people possible when your business was first starting out, growing your business gives you the opportunity to hire the best A-players. You'll need to hire professional management to succeed in this stage of your business, but prepare yourself that the transition for your team may be challenging.

Another challenge of adding professional management is that it can be difficult for you to let go of this part of the business. If you're like most entrepreneurs, a crucial part of your identity is wrapped up in your business. Bringing in professional management automatically puts a different stamp on the "personality" of the business and you may have difficulties letting that happen. If you choose not to bring in professional management, you are severely limiting how much your business can grow. It's rare that a business becomes a Fortune 500 (or bigger) company without a professional manager. It's a box you'll likely have to check before you can really leave the Acceleration Stage.

The Acceleration Stage is a stage you can go through multiple times. It's full of excitement, growth and new opportunities. When you focus your efforts on innovation, reinvention, integration, growing your business with professional management and transitioning to an investor owner, you'll make your way into the fifth and final stage: The Sustainable Stage.

9
STAGE FIVE—THE SUSTAINABLE STAGE

WHEN ENTREPRENEURS TRANSITION from the Acceleration Stage to the Sustainable Stage, they get a sense that they've finally made it. The success they've always envisioned (and other aspiring entrepreneurs have coveted) is becoming reality. The financial rewards are strong, and processes are refined and under routine improvement.

Reaching Stage Five, the *Sustainable Stage* is a monumental achievement and a cause for celebration. It's a tough road to navigate and few businesses manage to do it. When reflecting back to the elation and pure passion they felt when they were in the Intoxicating Stage, entrepreneurs now feel a sense of accomplishment, relief, pride and confidence. However, the business is not completely foolproof, so it's important that entrepreneurs not let that confidence turn into arrogance or complacency. It's important to not pause, not take a breather or get sloppy. Entrepreneurs need to keep the same intensity and focus that has gotten them this far, but channel the passion differently. Now is the time to lay a foundation for permanence and longevity, put evergreen solutions in place, and make plans for a sustained and profitable business. While temporary failures can always occur, knowing what to prepare for and monitoring the business for problems will drastically improve its chances of long-term success.

At this point, a business has two options: the business can thrive or it can fail. While it won't do either instantaneously, without proper nurturing and investing, it *will* do one or the other. There is no in-between. Businesses that fail are learning lessons that promote growth and improvement. Success and sustainability are not necessarily measured by the amount of revenue a business generates. To be sustainable and succeed, a business needs to be the best in its space, know its limitations and be very deliberate about its actions. And the entrepreneur needs to be happy.

> At this point, a business has two options: the business can thrive or it can fail. While it won't do either instantaneously, without proper nurturing and investing, it *will* do one or the other.

A business that has done a good job of this is Pasquale's,[62] an authentic Italian restaurant in western New York. It first opened its doors in 1975 serving only pizza, wings and subs. Its owners never intended for it to be a nationwide chain, but instead set out to be THE brand in small communities. They invested in the details of their small business—convenient parking, efficient take out and quality food—and have grown to three full-service restaurants. Now in addition to pizza, wings and subs, the restaurants serve pasta, seafood, chicken, veal, steaks and chops, offer a wide selection of beer and wine, and have a full-service bar. Pasquale's has grown, made money and accomplished their goals by knowing where they wanted to be and making a deliberate plan to get there. They aren't the largest revenue-generator in the restaurant business, but they are a small business success story. The owners are happy, they've had great market success and they've focused on maximizing their profit at each location. And they've lived a fantastic life!

Another successful business that made it to the Sustainable Stage is White Castle. White Castle's claim to fame is being the first fast-food restaurant in the world, with the first store opening in 1921. In 1961, it was the first fast-food restaurant to sell over a billion burgers. It was the first restaurant to use newspaper coupons; it was the first to apply the assembly line method to preparing foods in the kitchen and it even became part of a movie entitled "Kumar Goes to White Castle" in 2004 that was a huge hit, giving the restaurant a cult status. Its success can be attributed to always staying focused, always being open to innovation and always looking for new ways to market the business. And it has yet to franchise. There are 420 White Castle restaurants, all owned by the privately held White Castle Management Company.[63]

The restaurant industry is full of excellent examples of those that have made it to the Sustainable Stage and those that haven't. An example of one that didn't is Burger Chef, which was once the second largest fast food chain in the country after McDonalds. It peaked in the early 1970s with more than 1,000 stores, but its owner, General Foods, began to struggle. Some of the stores closed, some were sold to Hardee's and some of the remaining franchisees tried to hold on but finally closed in 1996.[64]

Another example of a restaurant chain that didn't make it was Cooker. Originally founded in Nashville but sold to a Columbus real-estate developer in the mid-1980s, Cooker prided itself on offering homemade dishes. It grew to 67 chain restaurants, but had moved away from its niche, resulting in decreased sales and declining customer loyalty. Cooker racked up about $70 million in debt. It filed for bankruptcy protection in May 2001, and in August of 2004, attempted to recapture its customers with significant interior and exterior design changes, and a new menu. It was not successful and had to close all of its remaining restaurants in three states in 2004.[65]

Examples such as these show us the challenges of becoming a sustainable business. In order for a business to grow and continue to succeed, entrepreneurs in this final stage must change the relationship with their business. They must turn the tables substantially and transition from employer owner to investor owner, as discussed in Chapter 8. They must accept their role as the leader or visionary of the business, no longer in the trenches performing the day-to-day responsibilities. Entrepreneurs in this stage must think about the business from the standpoint of improving shareholder value, improving the employee-employer relationship and improving the customer experience.

The irony of going through these five stages of business success is that you are never really done. If you have experienced all five stages and your business is growing and innovating, you will likely cycle through these stages more than once. Maybe not every stage, and maybe not in the same order, but the emotional part of the phases are sure to be experienced again as your business faces new opportunities and challenges. If you've hung in there and lived to tell about it, you will have developed business knowledge and character traits you didn't have before. You'll have a different type of confidence in your own ability. You'll have a better understanding of people and how they fit into an organization. You'll understand the value of values and not let the negative matters linger. You'll have faced challenges head-on, hired A-players as employees and have the right people in the right seats. You'll have embraced the hire-slow, fire-fast concept, making careful, deliberate choices in hiring valuable leadership team members and quickly recognizing those employees who don't conform to the business's core values. You'll have invested more time in the areas which have more risk embedded in them. And you will have laid the groundwork for deliberate living and relationships in your personal life.

If you've read this book and have followed my advice, integration and planned experience sharing will be a constant priority throughout all the stages of the business, and you will have a strong foundation for both by the time you get to Stage Five.

Entrepreneurs work hard to improve the lives of those who are most important to them, whether those individuals are in the business or outside of it. So often when I talk to business owners, I learn that the groundwork for deliberate living and relationships in their personal lives has not been laid. Many entrepreneurs realize that while their business is successful, they've failed to prioritize the most important things. Opportunities have been missed along the way, and attention and energy has been focused on the business instead of making it home for dinner with the family, watching the kids' sporting events and maintaining lifelong friends. If you find yourself in this situation, I believe it's never too late to start new habits and redefine priorities. It will require deliberate action and resetting priorities, but it can be done.

When you achieve Stage Five, all of your efforts become worth it. The key to true financial wealth and a happy lifestyle is having control over your own destiny. Making it to Stage Five means greater happiness, more freedom, more substantial wealth, and—what's equally important to many entrepreneurs—the chance to leave your mark on the world and make it something better than it was before you arrived.

10
STRATEGIES TO AVOID THE IMPACT OF FAILURE

THROUGHOUT THE FIVE stages of business success, there is always the threat of failure. Failure doesn't necessarily mean the business will go under, but a failure can have a different impact on the business, depending on what stage the business is in. As we discussed in the previous five chapters, failures are more detrimental in the Intoxicating and Trapped Stages; for example, when the business is new and less stable. They are less likely to have a huge impact in the later stages, such as the Accelerated and Sustainable Stages, when your business is more profitable and you have more experience and support to handle them. However, it's important to address the difference between temporary and permanent failures, and what you can do to minimize your risk of them.

When you lose a major client or key employee, or when you've experienced a personal setback that limits your ability to run your business, that's temporary failure. If a natural disaster damages your store or inventory and you don't have the right kind of insurance, that's also temporary failure (as long as you have the resources to get back on your feet). So is being cut out of the market by your competition, losing your customer base and experiencing significant employee turnover. Temporary failure occurs when your business—for whatever reason—isn't doing well and SEEMS it's either on the verge of collapse or in the process of collapsing, although that might not necessarily be the case.

In addition to the significant setbacks outlined above, there are a variety of smaller obstacles that can be just as damaging to a business if they're not corrected early enough. These problems are sneaky, and can undercut the business and your efforts in ways that are not immediately apparent.

I've experienced these setbacks and obstacles as a business owner, and many of my clients and peers have too. Here's what I've learned to do:

Grow (With Purpose) or Die

If you want to avoid failure, you must continue to grow your business. In the beginning stages of success, you may grow simply by having a better idea than your competitors, coupled with more enthusiasm and greater strength. However, that isn't enough to carry you through to greater and larger successes. Eventually your enthusiasm will wane and you'll need a clear plan for growth if you want to make it through.

As I discussed in Chapter 2, a written, deliberate business plan that includes action steps is essential to success. Without planning, you may find yourself unsure of what to do next. You may spend money, time and energy on things that either don't advance your overall goals for the business or actually detract from those goals.

Are you afraid that having a written plan will make you less able to take the business in new directions? You're not alone. Entrepreneurs are creative, innovative people, and many of us feel tied down and restricted by written plans. That's backward thinking. Written plans get you thinking about possibilities and give you a path to meet your goals. A written plan actually provides the underlying structure necessary to facilitate flexible and efficient decision-making.

Having a plan on paper for where you want your business to be tomorrow, next year and five years from now will help you recognize new opportunities when they arise. While your long-term goals will likely remain the same, your plan rarely will be executed as it's written, which is why reviewing your progress and reflecting on the adjustments you need to make to fully accomplish those goals are the most important parts of the planning process. You can review the written plan, see the progress you've made, and make modifications according to new priorities and conditions that come up throughout the course of a year. A written business plan gives you the basis for having conversations and making decisions about your future courses of action.

Think about professional athletes. The goal for each season is to not only make it to the Super Bowl or the NBA finals; it's to get that game-winning ring. So they draft and practice plays at the beginning of the season around what they think it will take to get them to that goal. Before each and every game, tapes are analyzed, plays are developed and adjusted, and the plan changes. This doesn't mean that the goal has changed. It simply means that they're going to have to go about getting there in a different way than originally planned. These adjustments are what make achieving these goals possible.

Amazon is a great example of a company that has adjusted its business plan to achieve its goals. When its website launched in 1995, Amazon was focused only on books. Its website read, "Welcome to Amazon.com Books!" and its mission was to offer "Earth's biggest selection and to be Earth's most customer-centric company." Now with Amazon Web Service catering to an expanded customer base, they add, "this goal continues today, but Amazon's customers are worldwide now and have grown to include millions of Consumers, Sellers, Content Creators, Developers and Enterprises. Each of these groups have different needs, and we always work to meet those needs, by innovating new solutions to make things easier, faster, better and more cost-effective."[66]

Uber has altered its business model to prioritize the safety of its riders and drivers. They continue to raise the bar with new screening technology, steps to reduce the risk of drowsy drivers, and safety features like an emergency button for the driver and rider that automatically sends key details to a 911 dispatcher.[67] Uber now delivers food from your favorite restaurants through Uber Eats,[68] provides a scooter option called JUMP bikes,[69] and has added a "Get to the Polls Button" so voters can catch a ride to the polls on Election Day.[70] Like Amazon, they've changed and adjusted their business plan to meet the needs of their customers and expand their business. The changes of their business plan always adhered to their value system and they had constant conversations about why the adjustments were warranted.

Be Flexible

Just as not knowing where you're going can lead to failure, so can being too rigid about your plans. Sometimes new ideas or new directions present themselves and if you won't let your business go where it wants to go (even if—*especially* if—it differs from your original idea), you risk stifling it. A systematic review of where you are today and what adjustments you need to make to accomplish your long-term goals are critical to achieving those goals. And sometimes opportunities pop up outside these reviews. As they do, be prepared to analyze them in relation to those goals.

Consider the Competition

Part of good planning is knowing and understanding your competition. How is your idea better than what's already out there?

What's new about what you're doing? Think big. Planning small may be your unconscious way of avoiding risk, but risk is an unavoidable aspect of starting a business. Knowing your competition will help you know—and sell—your idea better than if you act like you've created your business in a vacuum. Of course, one way to stifle the competition completely is to create a new market for your product or service. Look at what Steve Jobs did to the computing industry, what Google did to the advertising industry and how very light jets (VLJs) dropped the cost per hour in the aviation industry. (Read the book *Blue Ocean Strategy* by W. Chan Kim and Renee Mauborgne[71] for further clarity on this idea.)

Don't Listen to Naysayers

As I discussed in Chapter 5, most people can't understand the risks and rewards of being an entrepreneur, and some—out of their own fear and ignorance—will consciously or subconsciously attempt to dash your self-confidence and your dreams. If you want to succeed, you have to look past these people and forge ahead. If someone isn't interested in raising the bar or helping you take your business to the next level, move on.

How do you determine who is a naysayer? Consider who encourages you and provides positive challenges to your thinking. Encouragement doesn't mean being a "yes" man; in fact, encouraging relationships are often built between people who are conscious enough of each other's dreams and ambitions to offer healthy criticism. If someone isn't out to support you —if their ideas aren't meant to encourage you to tease out your ideas or to jumpstart you—the relationship is a dead-end.

And be very aware of the unintended naysayers in your life. These are the people who are coming from a place of care and concern who just don't understand why you would want to risk building a business from scratch instead of securing a job with an established company. Their intentions are not to sabotage you, doubt you or question your abilities, but their negative influence can be just as damaging.

Listen to your Advisors

While ignoring naysayers is a way to further your success, ignoring legitimate and helpful criticism can often lead to problems. Critique has its place and it can help you identify a problem or opportunity you wouldn't have seen. Ask your peers for advisor recommendations so you can secure the right advisor at the right time in your business to help you navigate through your temporary failure. If a professional advisor, team member, partner or encouraging mind individual with substantial experience in the topic speaks to you from a place of support, you should consider what he or she is saying and the implications of his or her suggestions. Sometimes solutions can be counterintuitive—I've seen entrepreneurs make the same mistakes over and over again. You don't want to make huge changes to your ideas, especially when you first launch your business, but you should always take suggestions under advisement. Learning from others helps us grow and can help push us into the next stage of success.

Safeguard your Emotional and Financial Resources

I discuss this in more depth in Chapter 11, but lack of spousal support can severely damage a business. If you put all of your emotional energy and resources into your business, you'll likely drain your life of key support. If your spouse or children work in the business, they need an emotionally safe place to turn to if the business fails. You have to safeguard people's emotional inventory of assets available to them.

Financially, as the business grows, you have to be very deliberate to diversify your risk and pay yourself properly. Pay yourself just as if you are paying any other bill. I advise you to deliberately pull money off the business balance sheet and put it on your personal balance sheet. There are two important reasons you need to do this. The first reason is it improves your liquidity situation and reduces your risk. The second reason is because if you leave all the money in the business, you might misspend it and not get a good rate of return on those dollars. Paying yourself allows you to diversify the risk of the business. While you can generally recover from complete financial ruin in ten years, if you don't have any financial resources left when you're faced with a temporary failure, you'll likely find yourself in a permanent failure situation.

Don't Overpromise

If you overpromise or overcommit to clients, employees or customers, particularly in your first years of business, you're likely to damage your reputation in a way that will prohibit future growth. Be realistic in what you can deliver. If you don't have the funds to provide twenty samples of a product up front, say so. If offering a certain benefits package to a potential key employee is too much for you to handle, offer what you can afford now with a promise to reappraise the situation in a year. And if you find you've overcommitted, apologize, correct your error and scale back to avoid issues in the future.

Overpromising can also put excessive stress on you and what you are overpromising might not even be that important to your customer. So do a really good job of only promising what you can deliver, because the physical, emotional and financial stress long-term can be incredibly damaging. Stress will win eventually if you don't control it. While it is important to push yourself and your business to reach new heights, sacrificing quality, performance or your own stress for initial sales is a sure-fire way to fail.

Have Fun

Starting and running a business is always hard work. It's stressful and it's usually exhausting, but it should still be fun. If you're overstressed and depleting your financial or emotional resources, you're probably not having any fun—a temporary failure that's sure to lead straight to permanent failure (and in record time) if left unchecked. Sometimes having fun requires deliberate intentional effort, especially if you're feeling stressed and not in a good mood. You need to have the right mental attitude. In the early stages of a new business, losing enthusiasm and drive can cause you to give up. And during the second stage, you'll need to keep up both your motivation and spirit, which requires a reinvestment of time and energy into yourself, your spouse and your crucial relationships outside of the business.

While it may seem contradictory, putting all of your energy, drive and time into your business can do more harm than good. We entrepreneurs are driven by our passion and enthusiasm to accom-

> If you commit to spending quality time with your spouse and your kids, and you set aside time to dream and think creatively at work, you'll be more passionate, more driven and more successful.

plish our dreams. If our dreams become just one more thing to finish, another joyless item to check off the list, we'll lose faith and give up. We'll discuss later how to keep your relationships strong while running a business, but know this: if you commit to spending quality time with your spouse and your kids, and you set aside time to dream and think creatively at work, you'll be more passionate, more driven and more successful.

I've talked about many of these strategies and suggestions in earlier chapters of this book. And while they are important strategies to practice when your business is realizing good times, they are even more important to practice when your business is going through bad times.

Types of Failure

The potential problems outlined above will likely present themselves in a variety of ways depending on your industry, your personality and your business's structure. It's helpful to recognize that you may experience temporary failures at one stage of success that weren't a problem at other stages. Different stages of success can—and will—foster obstacles specific to those stages.

Knowing the most common problems for each stage of your business's development can help you recognize and overcome that stage's particular problems—without experiencing a major temporary failure that could easily develop into a permanent failure.

Recognizing and Overcoming Temporary Failure

Learning how to succeed takes time. Many entrepreneurs have experienced temporary failure after temporary failure, without ever giving up entirely. They keep redesigning, reformulating, refocusing and in some cases, coming up with entirely new ideas. The trick to keeping a temporary failure from transforming into a permanent failure is first to recognize it and then to approach it correctly.

Do you view failure as a learning experience, something that can teach you what isn't working and what you can do better? Or do you view it as a *personal* failure, a mistake and a sign that you aren't cut out for success? Do you let your temporary failures push you to better yourself, your ideas and your business? Or do they make you lose faith and want to give up? Your attitude toward failure often makes all the difference in your potential for success.

That's the entire premise of John C. Maxwell's book, *Failing Forward.*[72] In it, Maxwell says that the only people who will succeed are the people who have a positive attitude toward failure. To get that attitude, you have to take responsibility for your problems and obstacles, challenge outdated assumptions, be optimistic, take new risks and persevere. Sound familiar? He's describing the entrepreneur!

First-generation entrepreneurs are uniquely qualified to view failure as a steppingstone for success, and the personality characteristics that lead one to "fail forward" are often the same personality characteristics that would drive a person to become a first-generation entrepreneur. And, since failure is a common occurrence when you start a business (or when you do anything worth doing), possessing the personality characteristics necessary to overcome those failures is a blessing.

Possessing the right personality isn't everything, though. You also have to approach your problems realistically and unemotionally. Take yourself out of the equation, while considering your obstacles objectively. This is called puzzle thinking.

Similar to lateral thinking puzzles, puzzle thinking is when you identify what the root problem is and brainstorm all the possible solutions to the problem, no matter how silly or ridiculous they may seem. For example, if you were to brainstorm ways to leave a room, you would consider obvious options such as using the door. With puzzle thinking, you would also consider throwing a chair through a window, drilling a hole through the drywall, or tripping the fire alarm so the fire department would let you out. Those might not be the most practical options, but the idea is to come up with as many solutions as possible without judgment. Then, once all of the options are on the table, go through them one by one, judge them and eliminate the ones that won't work. You end up with a handful of possible solutions to your problem that you might not have thought of otherwise. The puzzle thinking process forces you to think outside the box, which doesn't always come naturally to everyone. When you allow yourself the freedom to think without boundaries, interesting solutions present themselves.

In reality, our lives and our relationships with the people we care about are most important. They can make or break not only our businesses, but also our lives. Obstacles occur in business, but there's a better chance you can overcome them if the bigger picture is clear and you've prioritized your support relationships.

Temporary failures, even small ones, can harm your family, destroy your health, and devastate your finances if you're not able to recognize them when they arise, consider them thoughtfully and handle them rationally. Sometimes the obstacles are too great and the problems too many to continue the current venture. In those cases, you have to be able to cut your losses. And doing so in the right way at the right time will ensure you have enough emotional and financial resources left to try again.

In fact, most successful entrepreneurs have a number of temporary failures and busts behind them. While most first-time entrepreneurs have only an 18 percent chance of success, failure teaches you what not to do. Founders who have failed at a prior business have a 20 percent chance of succeeding on the next one, while founders of a previously successful business have a 30 percent chance.[73] Approached correctly, failure only brings you closer to success. And recovery from a doomed venture is usually easier than you think. Most people can return from complete financial ruin within ten years, and a failed enterprise can often make you refocus and realign your idea in an even better way, which puts you in a stronger position the next time you begin.

Perseverance is tough, but it pays off, as long as you learn from your mistakes and adapt your actions to make room for success. Henry Ford failed twice at automobile manufacturing, once as a manager for others and once in a company he started before he created the automobile he had always dreamed of—the Model A.[74] His third time was a success because he learned from his mistakes and changed his strategy.

Sometimes overcoming temporary failure is as simple as recognizing the need to hire a new team member or being flexible enough to take the business in the direction it wants to go—and not the direction you originally planned. Sometimes it's more difficult, and requires maintaining the gumption, enthusiasm and optimism needed to start again after a first, second, third (or more) attempts at success.

Knowing how to keep a positive attitude about failure and how to use it to increase your chances of success is essential if you want to overcome the temporary failures every first-generation entrepreneur experiences.

When It Isn't Temporary: Recognizing Permanent Failure

Permanent failure is when a person realizes he or she isn't going to be an entrepreneur. Permanent failure is not the complete failure of a business. As discussed previously, the vast majority of entrepreneurs start multiple businesses before one takes off and becomes a success; the failures of those first businesses are just a particular type of temporary failure. Permanent failure is something else entirely.

You'd think it would be very difficult to recognize permanent failure. After all, if most entrepreneurs start five, six, even seven businesses before launching one that becomes a success, how do you know when what you're experiencing is a permanent failure rather than a temporary setback? The answer lies in your available resources and in how you feel.

Entrepreneurs who are in the midst of a temporary failure (even one that destroys their latest or most recent ventures), all have certain things in common: they're still enthusiastic about starting a business, they plan to persevere, they view the current failure as a lesson learned that can benefit them the next time around, and they have the emotional and financial resources to start again. If two or more of the above are missing, you're almost always looking at a person who has experienced a permanent failure.

What factors contribute to keep a temporary failure from becoming permanent? Foster your financial and relationship resources. Set aside money for emergencies. Commit to nurturing healthy personal relationships. Surround yourself with people who add encouragement and support during difficult financial or professional times. And most importantly, vow to create and maintain a strong marriage and close relationships with your children and friends.

The role of these relationships both inside and outside of the business brings us to the final chapters of this book. These relationships are so important that I've dedicated an entire section to how each of them impacts the business and the overall happiness of everyone involved.

PART THREE
RELATIONSHIP
AND BUSINESS
INTEGRATION FOR
FIRST-GENERATION
ENTREPRENEURS

11
MARRIAGE

IT'S SEVEN O'CLOCK at night after a long day at work. You pull into the driveway, but don't get out of the car. The last conversation of the day is still playing through your mind—your executive team put off making a big decision because they wanted you to make it. You wanted **them** to take some risks and show they could figure it out for themselves—but they didn't have the courage, you didn't have the time, and now the deadline has slipped by and everyone's disappointed and angry.

Feeling frustrated and taken advantage of, you want nothing more than to go for a jog, take a hot shower and relax with your wife. Instead, you have just enough time to pick her up before meeting an important client for dinner. You breathe deeply and imagine pushing it all away to a place where you won't think about it anymore tonight.

As you wait for your wife to join you, you think, *I won't mention this to her. We've talked about my problems with my executive team a thousand times. It's been three years of stress and I don't want to burden her with this again. It'll only add to the pressure.* You take another deep breath, and decide to put the focus on her instead.

Meanwhile, your wife is preparing to meet your clients after a hard day's work. She's behind on an important project and the kids have done nothing but complain all day. Your eight-year-old son's teacher sent a note home that said he isn't paying attention in class. Your ten-year-old daughter is upset that all her friends have cell phones and she doesn't understand why she can't have one, too. Dining with your client is the last thing your wife wants to do tonight. She sees your car pull into the driveway and thinks, *I won't bother him with my problems. It's not a big deal. I can handle it.* But she's exhausted. She'd like to vent about her day, too, but doesn't think she can. *He's under a lot of stress,* she thinks. *We'll talk about all of this some other time when the business is on steadier ground.*

You watch your wife walk out the door. She shoots you a strained smile as she walks towards the car.

"Hi, honey," you say, as she climbs in beside you.

"Hi, babe."

You ask, "How was your day?" and she answers, "Fine. Yours?"

You respond with your own "Fine," And the twenty-minute drive to the restaurant is silent. You don't talk. You don't touch. Your internal monologues are in high gear, and the pent-up stress and anxieties continue to build for each of you.

Sound familiar?

The entrepreneur's relationship with the business and his or her spouse is complicated, to say the least. It's complicated because the entrepreneur has a connection to the business that is sometimes hard for the spouse to truly understand. How often do you hear about an entrepreneur selling the business to save a marriage? How many entrepreneurs are willing to or would be professionally satisfied to push aside their dreams of owning their own business to work for someone else? More often than not, the business survives and the marriage pays the price.

In a strong marriage, the entrepreneur will change his or her role in the business if it becomes necessary in order to remain happily married. There aren't many examples that I can think of where the entrepreneur pulls out of the business completely. So how can an entrepreneur and his or her spouse find harmony with the business, and stay married for the long haul? There is no easy answer, but this chapter will give you sound suggestions and advice that will lead you in the right direction.

For too many first-generation entrepreneurs—whether the entrepreneur is the husband or the wife (or both!)—the example above seems like daily life. What was once likely a passionate, loving and supportive environment has become a place of tension, resentment and grudging obligation. Communication, understanding and trust are all buried or completely absent. Fun is a thing of the past. Neither person is getting what they need, but they don't speak of it—let alone do anything to fix it. Life's daily stresses are eating away at the very core of the relationship and both spouses feel helpless to stop the cycle.

What happened? In short, lots.

You started a business—and maybe your spouse did, too. Worse, you might have started it or another venture while you were still single. You brought it into the marriage. And you brought your former habits as a single entrepreneur into the marriage with it. Single entrepreneurs have not yet had to tackle integrating a relationship with a spouse into the relationship with a new business. They tend to associate their "dream success" with social status and material conquests, and develop habits around those goals. To achieve that kind of success, it's probably fair to say that not many single entrepreneurs spend much time at home.

Business success is still tied to those goals for married (and married with children) entrepreneurs, but married entrepreneurs also have a core focus to provide for the whole family as opposed to providing only for themselves. Many married entrepreneurs have a self-inflicted expectation of the type of lifestyle they want to provide for their spouse and their families. For some, this might mean a big house in a nice community or membership to a club; to others, it might mean reputable schools for their children and grand family vacations to build memories. Nevertheless, there is an internal pressure—and possibly social and family pressure as well—to live life the way they always envisioned.

In addition, while the married entrepreneur is or should be dedicated to the family, the business may still be the true "core focus" for the individual entrepreneur. Conflicts with spouses can arise over all of these internal stressors. It can be difficult for both the entrepreneur and spouse to understand and navigate the internal battles.

The external battle is always about time. There's never enough of it. And it's worse depending on which stage of the business you're in. As your business changes and you enter new stages of success (and experience new setbacks), your relationship with your spouse and your spouse's relationship with the business will change—which will also create instances of and opportunities for conflict.

You remember starting your business, don't you? Maybe you're launching it right now. The first few years are extremely difficult. Intoxicating, but tough. You have superhuman energy, which you need for your extraordinarily hectic schedule and scale-tipping mental distractions, but you're hardly ever fully present with another person. (That's probably a big reason so many businesses are started by single people under the age of thirty.)

If you're married, one of the biggest frustrations for you and your spouse is that when you *do* have a few moments to spend together, it's hard for you to be emotionally available because all your mental energy and enthusiasm is tied up in getting the business off the ground. In the Intoxicating Stage, it's easy to appear absent from your spouse and family even when you're sitting across from them at the dinner table. Your spouse may think you don't care about your relationship with him/her, or feel resentful that you're exuberant and full of purpose about your business launch, but appear to not care much about what's happening in his/her life. Your spouse may feel ignored because of the long hours you work, and may be worried that money is tighter if lifestyle changes were made for the sake of your venture. Perhaps you think (because you're launching the greatest business ever!) that it's all about you. Maybe you're so wrapped up in yourself and your business—and so exhausted at the end of each day—that you've even stopped having sex.

I know it sounds extreme, but it's not. These are only some of the problems a spousal relationship faces when one or both are entrepreneurs. There's an interesting article by Meg Cadoux Hirshberg from the perspective of a non-entrepreneur spouse in her "Balancing Acts" column in *Inc.* magazine. The article, "Of Drivers and Passengers," or, "How Entrepreneurs' Families Cope"[75] discusses her life as the spouse of Stonyfield Farms' founder, Gary Hirshberg. These types of problems can take place at ANY stage of your business—even if you're entering the Light at the End of the Tunnel stage and feeling that you've overcome most of the hurdles you will encounter.

Consider this example of one first-generation entrepreneur:

After many years running a successful high-end kitchen appliance supply business from the position of top executive, this man decided to leave the company and start his own similar business. Like many FGEs, he had watched his employer's business from the inside and decided he could do it better himself. This was a few years after the real estate crash of 2008, which had caused even strong companies to suspend new investments and aggressively conserve assets. For the few years since then, no one was building houses or condos or starting home remodeling projects. As the tides began to turn, he realized there was a sizable, pent-up demand for his product. The timing couldn't have been better and he made good business decisions.

He negotiated for a fantastic showroom at an unbelievable rate and found the right manufacturers that were attempting to take advantage of his competitors' financial problems. He hired incredible talent at very low wages due to the unemployment environment and expanded his sales reach into an untapped market. With his years of experience, this man had deep knowledge and tremendously rich relationships to leverage. In his first year, he made more money than the vast majority of other first-year businesses.

But it was still less than what he made as an executive at his former company during the heydays of the late 1990s and his wife was worried.

They didn't talk much about their relationship since all they talked about was the business. Intimacy stopped because he came home so tired every night that he had no energy for sex. When he began entertaining clients and prospects every evening, his wife grew resentful that he wasn't home to help with their two young daughters. When they talked as a couple, it was usually in a heated argument because she couldn't get his attention any other way.

Ultimately, he couldn't lessen his wife's concerns. He considered bringing on a financial partner simply to please his wife. He disguised the true reason to others and created justifiable business excuses—a partner would give him "growth capital" and offer necessary "operational experience."

Taking on a partner would have been a disaster. The partner would not have brought anything to the table except money. Sure, that money would have flooded the business with capital, which the FGE thought could please his wife and ease the stress of their marital relationship. However, the FGE had no credible plans to deploy the capital to increase the returns of the business; in fact, he had no formal plans at all. He *did* have value in his rapidly and successfully growing business—it just wasn't yet producing enough cash flow. A capital injection would have greatly diluted that value.

If he'd taken on the partner, this FGE would have had to work even harder and longer to develop *more* business to satisfy a partner's return on the capital investment, and to pay for the increased overhead. In short, new capital would have meant MORE work, LESS money for the FGE and the partner, and MORE stress on the marriage! He had considered taking on a partner for all the wrong reasons.

The FGE didn't take on the partner. What did he do instead? He integrated. *They* integrated.

The FGE realized a universal truth of being a married FGE: your spouse is a vital part of your success and can impact it in a profound way. After that thought crystallized for him, he and his wife crafted a deliberately planned integration that they could adapt as their business grew. In my opinion, it's imperative for every married FGE to do this—it is absolutely essential to the survival of both the business and your relationship with your spouse.

Entrepreneurs can make both their marriage and their business thrive—and enhance the "fun" factor, too—by implementing a marriage integration plan.

How do you do it? Well, the first step is true for any marriage. You communicate.

Step 1: Communication for Married FGEs

I'll put my money on this comment: nowhere is communication more vital than within the spousal relationships of first-generation entrepreneurs. Every relationship requires communication to endure, but the unique stresses, personalities and life circumstances involved in the entrepreneur-spouse relationship make it an exceptionally necessary component. Without communication, there's no support. And, without a supportive environment, it's very unlikely that you're going to succeed—at home or at work.

Think back to when you had that first flash of insight, the idea for your business. Why did you start the business in the first place? It's hard work, and success isn't guaranteed—so why do it at all? Because you had a dream. Because you wanted to build a better life. Because you wanted to create something new. And of course, because it was going to be fun. Having an unsupportive spouse will not only drastically reduce the odds of your business's success, but will also contribute to decreased joy and fun on your combined journey.

In my own business, I counsel FGEs and their spouses, partners or significant others on integration of their business and personal financial lives. As you might imagine, this is quite a time-and emotion-intensive undertaking and we get to know our clients very well. Our initial meetings are with both the FGE and the spouse or partner, and are thought provoking, soul-searching hours.

Do you know what we almost always find to be true at the end of the onboarding process?

The FGE's spouse or partner usually has little idea what's going on with the business and not because the FGE is deliberately hiding or omitting anything. Sometimes the circumstances and cadence of a marriage can make it difficult to talk about the business, even when big things are going on. The FGE's spouse may be absorbed with family situations, transitions with the children or other personal life changes that distracts him/her from asking about the business. The FGE may choose not to bring up situations about the business because of everything else that is going on.

Granted, some spouses don't want to know. Some have no interest at all in the vinyl siding company's Cost of Goods Sold every quarter for the last two tax years. Some spouses do. Some fall someplace in the middle of wanting to know it all and wanting to know nothing except whether cash flow is healthy enough to live the life they want to live. None of these approaches are necessarily right or wrong.

If you're wondering what or how to communicate with your spouse about your business, then that's a very good place to start.

Step 2: Determine Your Shared and Competing Personal Goals

What kind of life do you and your spouse want to live? This should be one of the first topics you discuss when you're creating an integration plan for your marriage. Discuss it—and more importantly, write down your shared personal goals.

Spend time discussing your relationship and how to nurture it. When can you spend quality time together? How will you spend that time? What has to happen for both of you to be in the mindset of forgetting about external stressors and focusing on each other? Are there dream destinations or experiences you've always wanted to do together? When can you have the freedom to have fun together, be creative and do what you enjoy most? For some couples that may be laughter and for some it could be peaceful moments of silence. Determine together how you will connect in a way that is meaningful to your marriage and schedule a time to do it. You have to determine what your shared—and equally important, your competing—goals are to be able to move forward and grow together.

Competing goals especially must be expressed. If you don't talk about them, you can't make compromises, and neither you nor your spouse will get the things and experiences that matter most to you. If either (or both of you) begin to feel you have to give up too much for the sake of the business, the supportive environment that buoyed you when you first came together will quickly disappear. That's something you simply can't afford.

Take, for example, the case of a married entrepreneur who wants and needs to invest capital in the business at the same time the non-entrepreneur spouse wants to buy a newer and bigger house. What if they had never discussed these competing goals and there's not enough cash flow to do both? Who wins? Without communication and a plan about the couple's short- and long-term goals for the future, conflict will arise. If, however, the spouses communicate and align their desires for the future (invest in the business this year and save to buy a new house next year, perhaps), the success of both the business and the marriage can be assured.

It's easy to dismiss your day-to-day relationship with your spouse as a given, with a "we have a routine and it works for us" attitude that is not truly about clear and regular communication and understanding. It's easy to say goodbye in the morning and head off to your own separate days without each having a real grasp on what the other is engaged in from a long-term perspective. Life is busy. In truth, the daily relationships with your spouse— and with your business impact each other in momentous ways. If you can't share your excitement with your spouse, if you don't have a supportive partner to lift you up when times get tough, you won't be able to stay motivated. You'll quit looking forward to the day. You'll quit having fun. You'll quit dreaming. In the end, you'll quit—period.

You need to protect your marriage, and that doesn't mean sheltering your spouse from the business. We entrepreneurs often think we're doing our spouses a favor by not including them in the stresses of entrepreneurism, but this kind of daily shielding can lead to a total disconnect as to where the business is going relative to family needs. When our non-entrepreneur spouses also shield us from their daily stresses, we become disconnected at home. As shown in the example at the beginning of this chapter, when neither you nor your spouse knows what's going on in the other's world, conflicts begin.

For instance, a stay-at-home spouse may deliberately not share troubles the children are having at school or with friends. A working spouse may be overburdened by the household duties and child care activities that wait at home after a long day at work, but chooses to not burden the entrepreneurial spouse with complaints because both are working long, hard hours. Resentment builds, miscommunications abound and neither spouse confides in the other. The non-entrepreneur spouse never knows how the business is doing or where it's going, and the entrepreneur spouse is left out of important decisions at home. Worse, the entrepreneur spouse may never know the non-entrepreneur spouse is unhappy or beginning to resent the business until it's too late. Marriages end over such long-suffering resentment all the time.

It is no doubt a shared goal of all married people is to stay married. Seems like a given, right? Start there and move forward. Talk to each other. With that basis, you'll be able to create your list of shared and competing personal goals as a strong step in your marriage integration plan.

Step 3: Determine Spousal Role in the Business

Next, you must deliberately determine the role, if any, you want your spouse to have in your business and in the entrepreneurial adventure. Admittedly, it is a rare entrepreneur who thinks about this. Whether you like it or not, your spouse is a stakeholder of some sort in your business and even without an actual ownership in it, certainly has an interest in the business's success.

Consider your vision for the business. What does the future look like? How will you get there? Is there a role for your spouse in the plans? Does he or she have a talent for networking or accounting that you'd like to utilize and they'd be willing to utilize for the good of the business? Or, would you prefer your spouse have no role in the business at all? Once you decide what role (or non-role) you'd like your spouse to play, you have to communicate that desire to your spouse, as well as develop a process for continued communication as the business and your marriage evolves.

I've seen numerous iterations of spousal involvement with an FGE's business venture. The ones I've seen succeed are those where the spouse's engagement in the business is not static. Spouses and the business are moving targets, always evolving. There are times when a spouse may be knee-deep in the business, times when his or her role will change and times when the spouse may have nothing to do with it. You and your spouse must constantly be checking in and weighing what the business needs versus what the spouse needs versus what the family needs. You must have really good communication, and be honest about what is best for your business and for your marriage.

Say you've figured out that the role your spouse prefers in the actual running of the business is no role at all. That works—and it's great for you both. However, you still include your spouse in office celebrations, introduce him or her to key employees and key players in the business, and ensure they're acquainted with your partners and important clients.

Don't be mistaken that this is all you should do. You still need to talk to your spouse about what's going on in the business. You don't have to (and in many cases, shouldn't) include your spouse in the day-to-day decisions of the business itself, but you should share your goals and plans.

For instance, in order for your spouse to understand that you won't be home during the week for dinner very often, he or she needs to understand that your plans to expand the geographic range of the business include meeting with potential clients for dinner and networking after work hours. If you have plans to hire twice as many people in the next six months to accommodate the business's rapid growth, your spouse needs to understand that your emotional capacity may be strained for the next half year. If you're experiencing a new stress, such as the bank calling in a line of credit that radically changes cash flow predictions for even a profitable business, you must tell your spouse. Consider and communicate those issues that will cause you to be away from home more or that might distract you emotionally.

As someone who has lived this with my own spouse, I offer a cautionary tale. If your spouse does not have a role in the business and you're communicating about only these types of larger-perspective issues, don't make the mistake of crying wolf.

Talk about the realistic opportunities you have for the business. It is important to focus on what's actually coming up in the future as opposed to what you *hope* will happen. Often an FGE will land a meeting with a big client or a large investor—someone who could really be a catalyst for exponential growth—and then want to share the excitement with their spouse (*Honey, we got a meeting with McDonald's! Start looking at beach property!*) Sharing excitement is great, but if you include your spouse in your wishful thinking, you may find that he/she will lose faith in the potential success of the business when the meeting doesn't go as planned.

Many entrepreneurs think out loud. We dream big and often. If you want to keep your spouse's support, try not to share every hope or idea that comes into your mind. Like the boy who cried wolf, a pattern of hyping up the next big thing could easily work against you if your plans don't actually come to fruition. Too much enthusiasm and too few results will cause your spouse to lose patience. Then, when the real opportunity presents itself, he or she may discourage you from pursuing it.

While your spouse may be exceedingly supportive of even your wildest expectations, a history of sharing upcoming opportunities that don't pan out could lead your spouse to believe that business isn't going as well as you expected—which of course, can cause concern and undue stress. Instead, share high-level conclusions of your annual business-planning meeting. Don't talk about how great next week's meeting with a potential investor *might* go and the great things it *could* do for your business, because if it doesn't happen, you've created disappointment.

Instead, discuss with your spouse where you want the business to go this year and how you plan to get there. Keep him or her informed of what your plans are for the business in the next year, three years and five years. Be very careful how you present this information. You aren't seeking permission. You're informing your spouse of your plans and how this vision may impact your spousal relationship and the whole family. You're giving your spouse time and tools to reconcile the daily stresses and curveballs of the business with your long-term vision and goals.

Remember our kitchen appliance FGE who wanted to take on a partner to see an influx of cash flow to help alleviate his wife's concerns about money? If he'd sat down with his wife and had weekly conversations about his business's wins and losses, about what was on the horizon in terms of new opportunities and had repeatedly explained his cash flow plans (which were pretty good), he may have been able to alleviate his wife's concerns at the time. He didn't. And it caused them both a lot of undue stress and strain.

At the end of the day, he decided to not bring on the financial partner. With each of them at their own breaking point, the FGE realized he needed to help his wife understand where the business was and how it was going to improve. They implemented brief, daily discussions about what happened that day, what was planned for the next and what would likely happen in the following week—all in context with the long-term plan. To this day, they own a successful high-end kitchen appliance supply business and their marriage is fun again.

How did they do it? Through planned experience sharing.

Planned Experience Sharing

In Chapter 3, I introduced you to my concept of "planned experience sharing." I told you it's one of an FGE's strongest tools for success in business and life. And nowhere is it more important to implement than in your relationship with your spouse.

Scheduling time with your spouse is often viewed as unromantic, but it is, in fact, essential to keeping the romance alive. If you're not careful, your business will easily eat up all your time and mental capacity for others, including your spouse. If you want to keep your relationship vibrant, passionate and healthy, you have to deliberately plan and schedule "engagement" with your spouse, even if—especially if—you're exceptionally busy.

> If you want to keep your relationship vibrant, passionate and healthy, you have to deliberately plan and schedule "engagement" with your spouse, even if—especially if—you're exceptionally busy.

Schedule time for communication in the same way you might schedule a date night or a weekend trip. Make sure you *only* schedule time when you can be physically present and emotionally available. This is imperative. Your efforts will not achieve the desired effect if you're a million miles away and thinking about yesterday's board meeting.

Some of your planned experience sharing does actually have to be about the business. And you have to schedule time to talk about it—you can't do it effectively as the two of you are running out the door in the morning. Instead, sit down with your spouse on Sunday evening to talk about the coming week. Get out your calendars. Tell your spouse your short-term goals for the week, how you plan to accomplish them, any curveballs you're likely to encounter, and how that impacts when you'll be home and present and engaged. It's impossible for your spouse to support you in the unconditional manner necessary for your business's stability and growth on a day-to-day basis if you don't schedule this time and make it a habit. Your spouse needs to reconcile, possibly daily, why he or she is dealing with an absent partner for much of the week. Without regular, planned communication, trust can begin to erode—and trust is vital to any marriage. This is especially true for the marriage of a first-generation entrepreneur.

After setting up a ritual weekly check-in, remember to talk to each other every day! Ask questions, share your feelings and tune in your "listening ears." Say "Goodbye" and "Hello" every single day. Kiss your spouse. Be conscious of the fact that when you're talking to your spouse and are fully engaged, even if it's for five minutes and you're dodging distractions, you're able to make a significant connection with one another. Like most things in life, it's about quality, right?

If you have the more important basics of planned experience sharing down pat—daily, engaged communication and a weekly planning ritual—you're in a much better place for the big planned experiences to really mean something for your marriage long-term. You're already giving your spouse vital pieces of information that a supportive spouse needs to have in order to *stay* supportive and understanding (and not become resentful, or even hostile from a lack of communication). Now, you have delivered on any promises you've made.

Remember how you told your spouse you were hiring a new team and it would take about six months, and you'd most likely not be very emotionally available during that time? Well, when six months is up and your team is in place, take a break to invest into your spouse. Plan a long weekend somewhere your spouse loves and make the investment about *him or her*. It doesn't have to be a long vacation or an expensive getaway, but it does need to be an experience your spouse will cherish. Make the experience one hundred percent about your spouse. By taking a break to invest in your spouse, you will be acknowledging his or her importance in your life and ensuring your marital partner knows you're thinking about the relationship. You must be investing your energy, as little as you may have, into your spouse's emotional, sexual and companionship needs.

And you need to do this *at all stages of the business*—especially during the Intoxication Stage, when FGEs have a tendency to think it's all about them. While it may feel like that based on raw energy, everything is not about you—and if you learn to manage your unbridled enthusiasm in your relationship with your spouse from the very beginning, you're on your way to successful business and marriage integration.

When you're in the Trapped Stage, struggling with your own waning enthusiasm and the need to persevere, you want to have a spouse who's informed, engaged, appreciated and fully on board with your business journey. Remember, this is when your business might begin to experience temporary failures and an unsupportive spouse can easily tip the business's temporary failure into a permanent failure from which your business will never recover. If you developed a process of proactive communication and deliberate experience sharing throughout Stage One, then your spouse is aware of what you've already accomplished and your future goals, challenges and opportunities. A supportive spouse can help bolster your esteem and your energy, and will help you stay focused on why you decided to start your company in the first place. This could be all you need to push through to Stage Three.

By the "Light at the End of the Tunnel" Stage, many of your initial financial and business problems are resolved, and you may not have to work such long hours. If you've brought in extra help to reduce the amount of time you're physically working in the business, you might now feel that the business is on solid ground. The FGEs who do fail by this stage have probably failed in part from lack of spousal support, because their significant others have had to suffer through three to five years of long work hours, high stress levels and divided attention. If you and your spouse are experiencing this, now is the time to make a reinvestment in each other and your relationship. Invest in your spouse during this stage in new and different ways. Make him or her the center of attention.

You could plan a weekend for your wife and her girlfriends to go on a shopping spree or spa excursion **without** you. You could send your husband on a camping or skiing trip with his closest friends. Make it clear the weekend is about your spouse and only your spouse. Perhaps later in the year, you can plan a couples' romantic getaway to help foster communication in a different setting, as well as rekindle the sex life you had before marriage or in the early stages of your marriage in a fun, stress-free setting where the business is physically hundreds of mile away. It is absolutely critical that the FGE is one hundred percent present with his or her spouse during this weekend and does not think about business... at all!

The Acceleration and Sustainable Stages require a lot more strategic thinking, and you need to develop processes to ensure your business strategy is built with your personal goals—and the needs of your spouse and family—in mind as well. While it is critical to make "big" investments in your spouse during these stages, it is equally critical to demonstrate that planned experience sharing in smaller ways is still important in the normal routine and rhythm of your family life.

For instance, make it a point to come home for dinner every night even if you have to go back to work after dinner. Take the kids to school in the morning twice a week so your spouse can have the mornings free. Begin a new, shared activity with your spouse on a weekly basis. If you both enjoy dancing, take salsa or swing lessons one night a week. If you're foodies, take a gourmet cooking class together and plan to cook a meal together for the family once or twice a week.

The important thing is to show your spouse that he or she is important on a daily and weekly basis—and to create fun, engaging shared experiences no matter what stage your business is in.

At that point, consider where YOU are emotionally with the business. Are you happy where you are? Do you want to grow the business or acquire a new one? Is it time to explore the market to sell the business? Are you considering a new product line or taking the business in a new direction? These are all important questions in the final stages of success and if you want your marriage to continue happily, it is vitally important that you and your spouse are in accord as to what comes next.

While you don't need your spouse's "approval" to take the business in whatever direction you choose, you do need to communicate your thoughts and plans. The spouse needs to understand the consequences of your choices, how long your plan of action will last and how it will affect the family. Deliberate communication also gives your spouse the chance to voice concerns or objections to your plans, which may be added factors in your final decision.

One thirty-five-year-old entrepreneur, for example, was making a very good living from his twenty million dollar software development business when he decided he was bored and wanted to try to grow his business into a billion dollar company. He was extremely financially successful as it was, but his ego wanted more. He enthusiastically explained the plan to his wife who had lived through the first four trying stages of the business. Now that they were at the Sustainable Stage, she had no interest in what it would take to grow the business on a much larger magnitude—or to repeat difficult stages at the much, much faster pace necessary for the entrepreneur's plans.

It was a second marriage for them both and they had no children from it. He thought her ego would want to be a part of a tremendous American success story. At a minimum, he thought she would want to go along for such an exciting ride. He was wrong. She wanted nothing to do with the sheer work and stress associated with growing a twenty-one million dollar business into a billion dollar business, even if he could do it. She wanted him home for dinner; she wanted nice vacations where her husband was actually present; and, most importantly, she wanted a life with less stress.

When faced with such differing goals for the future, they decided amicably to go their separate ways. While the marriage didn't last, proactive communication ensured they both got what they wanted in the long run and helped avoid a messy, expensive divorce down the line. Later, the entrepreneur met and married a much younger woman one who had not lived through the first four difficult stages of the business's growth. His new wife was completely supportive of his goals and together they grew the business as he wanted (although they never did hit that billion dollar goal).

Conscious communication and planned experience sharing sound like strategic planning processes, right? Well, they are. The only difference is that it's a strategic plan with your spouse and family in mind. FGEs are notorious for avoiding a formal planning process for a variety of reasons: we don't have time; it's not how we think; it will hinder our business's ability to quickly adjust to opportunities and overcome problems. The reasons and excuses go on.

But even those who refuse to engage in strategic planning at work MUST do it at home. Entrepreneurialism can damage your marriage. If you have no plan to integrate your marriage relationship into your business and vice versa, something is not going to thrive. These methods will help keep your marriage strong in the face of the daily stresses that accompany starting and running a business, and will ensure your spouse understands what's going on.

Remember: an unsupportive or unhappy spouse can mean the eventual end of your marriage and your business. Deliberate, conscious, engaged, proactive communication and planned experience sharing will help ensure the continued success of both.

12
CHILDREN

How Entrepreneurism Grows Children

THE VAST MAJORITY of parents want to provide and do the best they can for their children so they grow up to be happy, healthy and independent adults. In many cases, a parent's decision to become a first-generation entrepreneur is, at least partially, based on the desire to have a "better life," even if the parent hasn't really defined what a "better life" means or what it actually looks like for themselves and their families. You may personally hope that a "better life" entails more money, more freedom and more time for enjoyment of quality family togetherness over the course of years. You must remember, a "better life" isn't a place you ultimately get to in some distant future after you've all paid your dues as an entrepreneurial family. It's a place you step into from the moment you make the decision to start your own business.

At the first step of your entrepreneurial journey, you're modeling life lessons for your children. Children don't need to be teenagers to understand that you or your spouse work for yourself instead of someone else who gives you a paycheck. Even a six-year-old can understand the benefit of keeping all the money you make instead of sharing it with someone else. Sure, that simple description is basic and full of exceptions, and you explain exactly what that means when they *are* teenagers. To a small child, you've shown empowerment, creativity, imagination, independence, ambition and a wealth of other positive attributes that they'll absorb and reflect on as they grow, because that's what children do. What better model to give them than that of an entrepreneurial spirit?

In my opinion, there are innumerable benefits to children that result from a parent's entrepreneurism. Aside from the spirit it imparts, it can also serve as a useful tool for teaching kids valuable life lessons, such as how to solve problems, how to develop a confidence that comes from independence and learning that everyone is important no matter where they are in the economic hierarchy.

In *Mind in the Making*,[76] author and researcher Ellen Galinsky, president and cofounder of Families and Work Institute, writes that perspective taking, critical thinking and focus are three of the "seven essential life skills that every child needs." Luckily, according to Galinsky, these skills can be taught. Even better, it seems the first-generation entrepreneur may be an ideal teacher.

Critical thinking is essential for reasoning, obtaining knowledge, and navigating the world in an intelligent and thoughtful manner. On page ten of *Mind in the Making*, Galinsky offers a particularly good exercise for parents to use in their efforts to teach their children to think critically. Galinsky suggests that when you're watching television with your kids, ask them what a particular commercial or advertisement is trying to sell and whether they think it's effective. Does it make them want to buy the product or service? If so, why? If the advertisement promises something, how could they find out whether the promise is something the advertiser can keep? As a first-generation entrepreneur, you can also use this exercise as a way to evaluate your own marketing efforts and to take on a new perspective—that of your children.

As Galinsky points out on page six of her book, entrepreneurs, marketers and other business people have to consider things from the customer's or client's perspective if they want to sell a particular product or service. This critical thinking is an essential life skill you can easily model for your children by simply including them in some of your brainstorming sessions. Depending on their ages, discuss your marketing plans with them at the dinner table or in front of them with other adults, or ask their opinion on whether your clients might use a new service or purchase a newly designed product. Again, even small children will surprise you with their deep perspectives, and they'll feel included, valued and loved in the process.

You're also modeling focus and drive for your children as an FGE. At any age, they can see the amount of time and effort you put into your work—most notably as a result of your time away from home. They know, because you tell them, that your time away is about work. They know that your work is what sustains them as a family—what puts foods on the table, gas in the cars, activities for them and quality-time family vacations on their calendars. And they understand it more and more as they grow. If you utilize some of the tips provided in this chapter about planned experience sharing with your children and engage with them deeply on a regular basis, they'll also grow to model the focus and dedication you've put toward your work as they navigate their own educational and life journeys.

Of course, there are downsides, too. Research on how children are affected by a parent's entrepreneurism is scarce, but what does exist suggests that an entrepreneur's kids are more likely to be affected by the negative aspects of starting a business than the entrepreneur. The results of a 2001 study by Chyi-lyi Liang and Paul Dunn[77] indicate that while entrepreneurs usually expect both they and their families will be happier after they start their businesses, those expectations are more likely to become truer for the entrepreneurs themselves than for their children. In fact, while the vast majority of the study's respondents reported increased personal happiness, only a little more than half thought their children were happier.

That isn't to say, however, that parents shouldn't start their own businesses. That same study uncovered that even though the majority of entrepreneurs said they didn't have as much time to spend with their children after they started their business, very few said their relationships with their children were strained and most (73.3 percent) said they believed their families would support their entrepreneurial efforts a second time. After all, most children know their parents are doing the best they can.

Integration with Children

Managing both parental and work roles effectively is harder for working parents than it's ever been in the U.S., including for fathers. According to Galinsky's research, men have been reporting increased difficulty in managing both work and family life since the 1980s. In 1977, only 34 percent of men said they experienced a conflict between work and family life. In 2008, 45 percent of men said they experienced conflicts. And in the 2017 Modern Families Index, half of the fathers interviewed said balancing work and family was an increasing source of stress, a third reported feeling burned out, and one in five said they worked after hours so they could spend time with their children.[78] The rising number of men who say they struggle with finding work-life balance means that men are more engaged in the family than they used to be. It also means that in two working parent families, neither parent feels they get to spend enough time with the children. The extreme time constraints experienced by entrepreneur parents make matters even worse.

Today, there are many types of family structures—long gone are the days when the majority of mothers stayed home to raise children and the Ward Cleavers of the world went off to work a corporate "suit" job from nine to five.[79] Parents today are married, single, widowed or same-sex partnered non-entrepreneurs and entrepreneurs who work in an office, remotely, or a combination thereof. There is no one-size-fits-all situation or solution when it comes to determining the quality and quantity of time spent together as a unit, or time spent individually with children. In that I am the only entrepreneur in my family, I speak from a place where only one of the parents in my household experiences the extreme time constraints of an FGE. My wife's time is obviously valuable, too—I say this simply to clarify the fact that my suggestions in this chapter come from a context of having a two-parent, one-entrepreneur family. I offer suggestions that have helped my family as an entrepreneurial one—and they might help yours, too, no matter what your family structure.

In integrating with children, the evil demon is still time and lack of it. Particularly in the beginning stages of business, entrepreneur parents are exceptionally overextended. They often feel guilty about their inability (or lack of desire) to make time to help the kids with homework or coach little league. In fact, time spent with family tends to be one of the first things to decline when an FGE feels overwhelmed by the demands of a new business. Even when time can be found, the entrepreneur parent is usually preoccupied—thinking about a pressing deadline or preparing for a crucial meeting—and is essentially emotionally absent. The reality is, though, that when you run your own business, you're unlikely to have as much time to spend with or as much emotional availability for your children as you did when working for someone else. Your business is an extension of you, and as such (especially at the beginning, when your enthusiasm for your new business is at its highest), your passion for the company will likely compete with your ability—and even your desire—to attend to your children's emotional needs.

This is even more pronounced if you're a single parent entrepreneur. As the sole care provider, you're responsible for all of your children's emotional needs as well as the daily essentials—getting them to daycare and school, grocery shopping and cooking, taking school-age children to sports and activities, and conducting nighttime rituals. How do you do all of this, in addition to performing the many, many tasks of running your own business? In my opinion, single parent entrepreneurs are likely more committed to building a different kind of life—one in which they can be home after school or when children are sick. One in which you can travel together during summer vacations and build lifelong family memories. That extra commitment often means you're able to persevere through tougher odds. What might make one entrepreneur quit will cause you to work even harder because you don't have a choice. You know what kind of life you want to build for you and your kids, and entrepreneurism is your ticket to that life.

Thankfully, being an entrepreneur—whether a single parent entrepreneur or a married entrepreneur with kids—doesn't mean you or your children have to resign yourselves to a less-than-ideal family environment. Your kids aren't destined to play a smaller role in your life just because you wanted to work for yourself. As discussed in previous chapters, the trick to a supportive and happy family lies in *deliberately* planning how you spend your time in order to best serve your current needs and your goals for the future.

If you haven't been practicing planned experience sharing, now is the time to start.

Planned Experience Sharing with Children

Whether you started your business as an FGE at about the time you were beginning a family (which is basically the same as giving birth to twins, so good luck!), or when your children were older and school

> As an FGE with children, you'll have to learn to respond to the changing needs of your business and children— often at the same time.

age, you've created two very important parts of yourself. Both avenues of your life will grow and change over time, as will your roles along both paths. It would be significantly easier to handle these changes if they occurred in isolation, but life is rarely so compartmentalized. As an FGE with children, you'll have to learn to respond to the changing needs of your business and children—often at the same time.

Where do you start when you're considering the management and integration of your time? Remember: you must practice conscious communication and planned experience sharing. You must communicate with your spouse, if you're married, in the form of regular calendaring events and daily check-ins about when you expect you'll be home to help with diaper changing or activity-shuttling—whichever phase you're in. Whether you're a dual working parent family or a single parent, you'll need to communicate often and actively with your caregivers. Advance planning and communication each week eases everyone's task load and helps prevent surprises—or at least makes the occasional overtime surprise more palatable. You must also communicate with your children if they're old enough to understand that you're at work when you're not home. Include them in the calendaring meetings and daily chats. You don't need to mire them in the details—just let them know when you'll be there for them.

Then plan the experiences you'll have with your children. Before entering an item on your to-do list or scheduling a meeting or event that keeps you away from home, consider the item or event's purpose. Remember: You should mentally calculate how it's going to help your business in the short or long term and what affect your absence from home will have on your children.

When I began to contemplate how absences in the name of growing my business would affect my wife and our three children, I started to think about my role as my children's father at different stages of their childhood—and tried to make my time with them provide what they needed from me then. It makes sense—as children get older, their needs change and our roles as their parents must necessarily change as well. An infant's needs are substantially different from the needs of a teenager. Even a toddler's needs differ from those of a preschooler. We have to be a different parent to our children throughout it all.

Erik Erikson's *Theory of Psychosocial Development*, first published in 1950, has been a leading resource in child development for decades. The theory provides that there are eight stages of life leading from birth to old age, and a child must pass through FIVE of them by the time he or she reaches adolescence! That's a lot of developmental stages in a short period of time and a lot of pressure on parents to get it right as best they can. Erikson says that if the challenges in each stage are met, the child passes into the next stage with a healthy sense of self and trust in others. If not, he or she will continue to struggle with that particular conflict indefinitely.[80]

Infants and toddlers need near-constant attention to keep them safe and healthy. According to Erikson, an infant mostly needs love and support, and to have his or her needs met on a consistent basis. As an FGE, the best-planned experiences you can share with very young children are to hold and talk to them every day. People always told me that working is easier when children are that young, as long as you're there every day to hold them and solidify your bond. If your business launch is taking your time into the evenings, plan to come home for dinner and hold your infant before it's time for sleep. An infant's bedtime is usually early, and there's plenty of time in the evening to work from home or go back to the office. Let your baby hear your voice, smell your scent and feel your touch.

Toddlers, according to Erikson, require strong parental guidance in order to develop a sense of self-esteem and personal will. This is because from about eighteen months to three years of age, children learn that they are individual people with the ability to make their own decisions. And as all parents know, toddlers are intent on making their own decisions.

During this time, parents need to guide their child's behavior gradually, firmly and with love, praising the child's attempts at independence. If parents react in a firm yet loving way, the child will develop a healthy sense of autonomy and willpower, which will help develop self-esteem in the coming years. If the parents are too harsh or too lenient, the children will become ashamed of their attempts at independence and doubt their own ability to make decisions. This could lead to obsessive or impulsive behaviors later in life.

In many cases, a busy parent who isn't home enough experiences the urge to be either too indulgent or too restrictive with the kids. Because she isn't home much, an entrepreneur mother may think she needs to be extra firm when she's at home so that her children learn her expectations. Or, an entrepreneur father may not want to discipline his children during the precious moments he gets to spend with them and so becomes overly permissive. An entrepreneur with a toddler at home must resist these urges and strive to provide the strong but loving guidance that a child needs in order to develop into his/her own person.

When you're considering how your absence because of work will affect your kids at this stage, keep in mind that the time you schedule to be at home to interact with your child needs to also include time to check in with your spouse. Ask if your spouse has noticed a pattern of overindulgence or excessive authority coming from you. Help keep each other on an even keel by developing rules and methods of discipline that you both follow all the time. Share that with caregivers. This will help your toddler learn rules and expectations, while also keeping your own conduct consistent. When you're sharing precious time with your whole family or just one-on-one with your toddler, your child will understand your expectations.

During the preschool years, parents serve as first-level educators, providing their kids a variety of opportunities for learning and creative thinking. While an FGE is unlikely to have large blocks of time to spend with the child during the weekdays, you can make time after dinner for quiet time with age-appropriate books and toys. Make sure that you're home to read them a story at bedtime (and if you're not, do it over the phone, or video chat). Weekends are great times to set aside a more substantive chunk of time for trips to the park, library and other activities that encourage social interactions.

And kids are never too young to take to the office! Make a habit of spending special time with your preschooler where you work—even if it's to pick up a doughnut on the way and stay only fifteen minutes to check email. Your child will see and absorb this part of you. Do you have seasonal weekend networking events? Are any of them family friendly? Take your child to the morning tailgate for the college football game. You will have integrated spending time with your child with completing a task for work and everyone wins.

In my opinion, parenting gets more complicated as children get older. School-age kids need daily help with homework, rides to extracurricular activities, assistance with school projects—and they need *lots* of emotional support to help them take on new responsibilities, handle defeat, and deal with changing social and societal pressures. It's also easier to spend time with them when they're older. They're self-sufficient, interesting people with their own thoughts, dreams, goals, concerns and frustrations—things they want to share with you. How you help them handle their growth will affect your relationship with your children and mold how they view themselves as individuals.

No matter how old your children are, you always want to spend time with them. After all, you wouldn't have chosen to have a family if you didn't. So you need to plan—and plan well. Without proper planning in the first two stages of success, your busy schedule will most likely prohibit you from having the time to participate in many of your children's day-to-day events and extracurricular activities—in fact, you'll probably be the most time-strapped you're ever going to be in any stage of your business. And the unfortunate truth is that most FGEs don't *make* the time to engage in precious family rituals because of it.

However, you must. There are always ways to make your children feel important, loved and supported, and they don't have to take all day. The amount of time you spend is much less important than the kind of time you spend. Only have an hour one day? That's enough to make a satisfying connection with your child.

Think of all you can do in an hour. Go home for dinner, even if it means you have to return to the office or work later from home. Go home after a dinner with clients and read your preschooler a bedtime story, or grab a basketball or the bikes and play. Watch a sports practice from the sidelines. Take your child for a drive. Just talk. Dedicate longer Saturday afternoons to family fun—swimming, time at the park, museum trips—anything at all developmentally appropriate and fun for your children.

In my own life, I used to routinely experience tremendous anxiety on Sunday nights over beginning the work week (and I would bet that many FGEs do). It got so bad that my Sunday nights were almost sleepless and peppered with crazy, nonsensical thoughts. Monday was always bad because I'd convinced myself the night before that it would be.

Then, an idea hit me. I planned a very early restaurant breakfast with my three kids for the following Monday morning. Monday came, my kids and I got up and we had breakfast together. We had time to eat, talk and be together. I took them all to school and then went to work. Now on Monday mornings, my kids and I have precious time alone together and my wife has a kid-free morning, starting off her week with some rare alone time and the ability to focus on herself. And best of all, I no longer have anxiety on Sunday evenings about the busy week I have on my schedule as an FGE.

In later stages of business success, you'll likely be dealing with big-picture strategies and working hard to expand your business into a large-scale success. While time is still tight, you will have hired people to help manage the business's day-to-day activities, and will likely also be able to schedule some time away without worrying that the business won't function at its best in your absence. You're also likely to have increased cash flow, and could have the money and time to take a family vacation. As cash flow increases, be deliberate in creating experiences with your family, even if it's only spending one day hiking or two days fishing. The experiences don't have to be extravagant. They *do* have to be meaningful.

Networking or professional conferences are an ideal way to integrate work and meaningful experiences with your family. Conferences are often held in resort-like locations. If you're attending a week-long conference, extend your stay and have your family fly down to meet you during the last day or two. They can run around on their own while you wrap up your conference and then you can all spend a few days on a family vacation.

As you can see, it doesn't take much to have high-quality interactions with your children. Your time together doesn't have to be time-intensive or cost much. Regular, predictable interactions with your kids will enhance communication, and build trust between you and your children. Whatever you plan, the most important thing is to make sure your children feel valued and know that you're always there for them when they need you.

Remember that by modeling a well-integrated business and personal life yourself, you're teaching your children lessons that will enable them to succeed in all areas of their lives without feeling forced to give anything up. While there may be times when you don't get as much time with your children as you'd like, planned experience sharing and mindful prioritizing will help bring you toward your future goals in a family-friendly way. And, don't worry: even when you suffer the occasional obstacle to your plans, your children will likely still be supportive.

After all, you're the parent, and your children love you.

13
PARENTS

THE RELATIONSHIPS WE have with our parents are perhaps the most complicated relationships of all. We've loved them and hated them. Embraced them and rebelled against them. We've disappointed them and made them proud. They were our biggest cheerleaders, our harshest critics and sometimes both—simultaneously. They raised us, fought for us and punished us. Most importantly, for good and bad, they helped create us. Those identities affect who we are as entrepreneurs.

We already know that entrepreneurs are different from other people. Our visions are larger. We want more: to do more, be more, have more. As children and young adults, our parents probably thought of us as people who seemed driven to take the hard way and make things more complicated than necessary. They may have felt we expected too much or took too many risks. In truth, whether our parents understood us was likely tied to whether they themselves were entrepreneurs.

Research shows that children of entrepreneurs are 60 percent more likely to become entrepreneurs themselves.[81] Children of these entrepreneurs are often raised with the idea that starting a business is both doable and worthwhile. They're typically raised to take charge, be self-reliant and go for their dreams. They did, of course, have problems (most parent-child relationships are complicated), but the problems between entrepreneurial-minded children and entrepreneurial parents are unique.

They may disagree on whether the adult child entrepreneur should start his or her own company in a different (or competing) industry, or whether the adult child entrepreneur should take over the parent's enterprise. Sometimes, a parent's previous failure may influence the degree of support he or she gives to the adult child entrepreneur in later years. Still, it isn't usually difficult to get an entrepreneur parent to understand why an adult child would decide to strike out on his or her own, and the adult child entrepreneur of an entrepreneur parent usually feels understood.

The other 40 percent of entrepreneurs are first-generation entrepreneurs like you. FGEs may have parents who offered support, or they may have parents who told them their dreams were unrealistic. Regardless of later support, children of non-entrepreneur parents are almost always told, at least at first, to get a "real job." This is particularly true in the United States, where 72.2 percent of parents believe the current job market should play a role in their children's career decisions.[82] In that kind of mentality, stability comes from a good-paying position inside someone else's company, not from striking out on your own in a high-risk, high-stakes venture.

At first glance, the non-entrepreneurial parent's message seems at odds with the "American spirit." Americans hold tight to stories about successful entrepreneurs. We love to hear rags-to-riches tales in which self-starters pull themselves up by their bootstraps and make something for themselves. It fits into our self-image as a nation of cowboys and pioneers. Strangely enough, however, non-entrepreneur parents in the United States don't want their children to be entrepreneurs, at least not consciously.

From the time we're very young, we're told that the path to success is to study hard, do well in college and land a steady, good-paying job. Those of us who decide to do things differently, those of us who want to create something for ourselves, those of us who want more, are often looked at strangely. Our parents may even try to dissuade us from taking what they feel is a risky

> Those of us who decide to do things differently, those of us who want to create something for ourselves, those of us who want more, are often looked at strangely.

and potentially unrewarding route, no matter how badly we want it. At its worst, parents may be our most outspoken naysayers in the first stages of our fledgling business.

Once we're conventionally successful, of course, that all changes. Suddenly, even if they weren't before, our parents become extremely supportive and exceptionally proud. They want to brag to everyone and talk about what an amazing life we've created for ourselves. We become their shining stars, even if at first, we were considered foolish and they tried everything they could think of to dissuade us from pursuing our dreams.

Unlike second or third-generation entrepreneurs, those of us who are FGEs may feel the need to make our parents understand and approve of our choice to become an entrepreneur. This quest for understanding may turn out to be one of our greatest struggles.

As I mentioned in earlier chapters, I was raised in a non-entrepreneurial family. When I was preparing to graduate from high school, the expectations were that I would go to college, major in something that would provide a good living and get a job. My mom was concerned about the risks of me starting my own company and so was my step-dad. He worked for a large, global engineering company where everyone from the laborers to the engineers were highly skilled, and had technical and advanced degrees. My step-dad and his friends were on my side and wanted me to win, but they had an initial adverse reaction to my becoming an entrepreneur. It was so far away from what they could possibly do or understand.

In most occupations, such as becoming an engineer like my step-dad, there is a clear career path. You go to college, get good grades, maybe attend graduate school and get a job. The same is true for the medical field, which requires an undergraduate degree, medical school, residency training and medical licensing. There is no clear path to becoming an entrepreneur. There's no right, wrong or set way of doing things because it can be done a number of different ways. That can be a very difficult concept for non-entrepreneur parents to wrap their arms around and support.

Now that I'm a parent, I've definitely raised my kids to be independent and consider all of their post-college options. We've talked about it since they were young and we still talk about it now. Unlike me, my kids have grown up with entrepreneur families around them. They have been exposed to the lifestyle and recognize the economic and flexibility differences that come with starting a business, but they've seen the stressors and challenges too.

When they were younger and we would walk into a business, they would ask me, "Dad, do you think this is a good business and if so why?" Now that they've gotten a little older, when we walk into a business, I ask them the same thing and enjoy hearing their observations and opinions. If they have a negative customer experience with a business, they talk about it and wonder what the root of the problem is.

Although I am an entrepreneur, I've been careful to balance both sides and encourage my kids to do what they feel called to do. I've pointed out that they can still have a great career working for someone else if the entrepreneurial life is not for them. And I don't think all of my kids will be entrepreneurs. In fact, if I had to guess today, I'd say I might have one child who chooses that path. Whatever they choose, they have grown up to be aware of their options, unlike most children in our country. They are not opposed to getting a traditional job, but they recognize there is a whole world of alternatives out there available to them.

It is important to remember that this is your life and your dream. If you have supportive parents, wonderful. If you have loving parents who don't understand your career path and therefore don't support you, that's okay too, as long as you can hold fast to your goals and your ideas in spite of them. It may be helpful to remember that even the most opposed parent likely only wants what's best for you. An unsupportive parent may be afraid you'll get financially and emotionally hurt. They may not believe you'll be able to recover from a failure. In short, they're afraid.

If you want to ease their fears, you might consider sharing your plans with them. Don't just tell them you're starting a business—tell them why and how. Invite them to your business launch party, or social networking events around the growth of your business, and introduce them to your staff and to clients. Get them excited if you can, but don't ask for permission. If you still can't get support, take their criticism with a grain of salt. Hear it—integrate it—but don't act on it.

Remember: particularly in the early years, movement through the stages of success depends heavily on your ability to stay motivated and driven despite the criticisms of the naysayers. Carry on with your plans, and garner support from your friends, your spouse or significant other and your professional networks. Your parents will probably come around eventually. If not, don't take it personally. Some people just don't have what it takes to dream big. Build the life you want, the way you want. Even if they can't say it, even if they don't know it, that's really what your parents would want you to do anyway. It's your life. Reach for more.

14
FRIENDS

Entrepreneurs and Friendships

THE RELATIONSHIPS WITH our friends can be some of the most beneficial, enlightening and important relationships we have, both personally and professionally. Unlike family members, both parties in a friendship volunteer to be friends with each other. Each friend must selfishly benefit equally in order for the friendship to be successful, rich and most importantly, long-term. Each person in the relationship must get something out of it that they perceive as being fair and equal, and what that is depends on what's important to the individual. Successful friendships can mold and influence a person's values, perspectives, and attitudes in permanent ways because successful friendships require a positive investment of energy and effort. Bad friendships will

> While friendships can have a wildly profound and positive impact on your life, they're also the first relationships to be cast aside when we're faced with the intense time demands of running and growing a business.

simply die because they're not win-win—which is sometimes easier than enduring a stressful familial relationship that's permanent.

While friendships can have a wildly profound and positive impact on your life, they're also the first relationships to be cast aside when we're faced with the intense time demands of running and growing a business. There's no doubt that having two or three unconditional friends results in a longer, happier, more fulfilling life. The Harvard Study of Adult Development has been following the same group of men since 1938 to find out what factors lead to happy and healthy lives. They were expecting to find factors like cholesterol levels or physical activity to have the greatest influence, but instead they've learned that having strong personal connections with other people is what leads to overall happiness, better health and more contentment.[83]

For most first-generation entrepreneurs, it is critical to nurture and grow those unconditional friendships which can (through the various stages of your business) help produce phenomenal personal and professional results.

By now, you're likely familiar with the key to relationship success. Whether it's a relationship with a child, a business partner, a spouse, a parent or a friend, the key to a lasting, successful relationship is planned experience sharing. Think about friends. Who's really there for you? Time is a precious commodity for entrepreneurs and if we want to spend it wisely, we need to invest in the people who are willing to invest in us. Which of your friends are always there for you with a word of encouragement or a new perspective? Most people are lucky to die with two or three unconditional friendships. Who are yours? If you can't think of any friends who truly support you, don't pour your precious, limited time into people who aren't going to be there for you, or who actively negate or attempt to deride your passion and your dreams. Make new friends.

You will find throughout your entrepreneurial journey that your best friends likely will be other first-generation entrepreneurs. Yes, you'll have your old high school or college roommates as friends. Sometimes, they'll understand you and what makes you an FGE. Sometimes they won't and your relationship will change. Many FGEs report that they grow apart from their pre-entrepreneurism friends when they start their own businesses because there's no longer much to talk about but old memories. If you're a parent, you'll likely make new friends who are parents of your children's friends. That works for a lot of people, but you might find it difficult to connect with them if you're already pressed for time and can't attend a lot of the activities where parents socialize and make new bonds with other parents. Without time or an FGE connection with new friends, you might feel like you don't fit in.

So who understands the problems you face as a FGE? Sometimes old friends and new friends can try, but they can't truly understand the pressures that surround making payroll or selecting the right branding firm to rebrand your company. They can't fully comprehend the intense pressure of firing a founding employee because that person has not grown with the business. Other FGEs do understand—and they understand it well.

Some of your best friendships may be born as a result of networking and social events dedicated to people like you. As I've noted, there are plenty of organizations such as the Entrepreneurs Organization, Young Professional Organization, your local Chamber of Commerce, Rotary and Kiwanis where you'll find an abundance of like-minded people.

What can you do with old friends and new friends worth investing in? You have to use the planned experience sharing process to figure out how to keep them. Chapter 3 discusses planned experience sharing in detail, and how I practice and prioritize it in my own life.

Mixing Business and Friendships: FGE Caveats

As time goes on, you might consider including either older (longtime) or newer entrepreneurial friends in your business. Be careful. There is no "silver bullet" formula for how to include friends in your business. Determine where and if you want them to be a part of the business—as a sounding board, as an investor, as an employee or as a partner, if at all—before you talk to them. Write down your expectations for the inclusion and clearly articulate what you want from them. You should also formulate a written exit strategy for if, or when, you need to exit the professional relationship in order to maintain the friendship.

One of the most common forms of business collaboration is friend as investor. If you find your business in the circumstance where you're raising equity to finance your enormous growth on the way to a major liquidity event, it's natural to want to include your friends and family in that equity offering so "they can come along for the ride." Obviously, before doing so, you must consider all possible alternatives to this outcome. How would you feel if the equity raises were a colossal failure because of *future* equity raises that dilute early investors? How would you feel if the acquiring firm of your eventual liquidity event negotiated an enormous package for you, but radically diluted the other shareholders?

To the extent you want to include your friends in a financing package for your business, consider having your investment advisor or legal counsel explain the risks to your friends on a formal basis. In addition, consider insisting that your friends' legal and tax counsel weigh in on the investment. At a minimum, your friends will have been very well informed and would have had plenty of opportunities to decline the opportunity in a professional manner.

Occasionally, you will have the opportunity to hire your non-entrepreneur friends. Often, the match looks made in heaven—on paper. You implicitly trust your friend, you assume he or she will work hard for your company and your friend possesses a skill or talent your company desperately needs. Unfortunately, while there is the possibility that the friend-as-employee relationship will be a win-win for everyone, it's extremely unlikely that it will actually turn out that way. You should be prepared for the fact that your friendship will change—sometimes drastically—and that in most cases, it will be for the worse.

If you hire your friend as an employee, you'll learn that you will have to hold your friend to the same standards at work as the rest of your employees, even if you don't want to. Your friend might take offense that he or she is not receiving preferential treatment, which would certainly put a strain on the professional relationship—and perhaps the friendship as well.

If you decide to hire a friend, you should commence the professional relationship in much the same way as you would when bringing a friend on as an investor. Have clearly-written expectations. Write down potential problems and formulate written strategies for dealing with those problems. Consider an employment contract for your friend, if only to test the ability to negotiate a business matter without straining the friendship. If the friendship is important to you and you find you have conflict during these negotiations, take a very serious look at continuing the process. With open communication and transparency, it is possible to make the friend-turned-employee relationship work.

Erik Roemer is my Chief Compliance Officer and has been working for me since 2000. We were great friends in high school, lost touch through college, then reconnected when he and his wife moved back to Columbus in the late 1990s. He was looking for a job and I needed someone with his expertise. Before I hired him, we had very candid conversations around expectations, and how we would handle the work relationship and our personal friendship. We agreed the business would come first, even when times were tough. Although he's never said so, I'm guessing there were times when he didn't like me very much as a friend, but because we have a fundamental respect for each other, we made it work. Our kids are the same age and when I see him outside of work, we have fun together and don't talk about work. Our friendship changed, but in my opinion, it's more robust than it was before. It's been a successful relationship because we communicated, figured out ahead of time how we would deal with problems and put the business first.

A friend-as-employee relationship is one type of challenge, but a business partnership between two friends is another. When two friends enter an active business partnership, problems often arise when there is no business plan, no continuity, and no alignment of where they are trying to go with the business and why. In my experience, nine out of ten business partnerships blow up. When they do, it can be messier than a divorce because there is usually no prescribed exit agreement. Sometimes there are complicating factors tied to it as well, such as economics, egos, family members involved in the business or questionable business decisions. In the entrepreneurs' defense, sometimes they don't know where they want the business to go when they are first starting out. The sad reality of a business partnership falling apart is not only does the business go down in flames, but the friendship does as well.

The point of this is not to suggest that you should or should not hire your friends; rather, to ensure you understand that your relationship will change once you become employer-employee. To make sure you don't lose a good friend, you have to ferret out as many potential issues and problems as soon as possible—preferably before the business relationship actually commences. If you take the time to do this, you dramatically increase your odds of coming out with a win-win situation. Much like my situation with Erik, there are plenty of examples where old friendships made the greatest business relationships.

CONCLUSION

The journey of a first-generation entrepreneur is exhilarating, stressful, rewarding and other emotions just too many to list. You'll have good days, bad days, frustrating days and everything in-between. Whether you are just launching your business, are knee-deep in the growth or thinking of your exit strategy, I don't have to tell you that challenges as an entrepreneur—a first-generation entrepreneur specifically—are unique. You either have begun to experience it yourself, or have a better understanding of what to expect now that you have read this book.

The FGE's five stages of business success may be neatly packaged in separate chapters, but there is nothing neat or predictable about them. The fact is, while the descriptions are accurate and true, the stages are messy. There's no one right way to go through them and you will likely experience them more than once. Not necessarily all of them in the same order or with the same intensity, but you will probably see them again. Each time, you will have more stamina, experience and ammunition to succeed.

Along the way, you need to remember to prioritize the most important relationships in your life and nurture those relationships along with your business. Whether you have a spouse or significant other, children, friends, parents or any other relationship worth maintaining, you should use the integration and planned experience sharing tools described in this book to keep the peace, harmony and overall life happiness. Theodore Roosevelt said, "Nothing worth having comes easy," and that couldn't be truer for the first-generation entrepreneur.

One thing that FGEs may experience that multi-generation entrepreneurs or traditional business owners don't is loneliness. Despite the fact that FGEs are surrounded by people to talk to all day—employees, vendors, suppliers, customers, family and friends—FGEs may feel very much alone. They take risks alone, make unpopular decisions alone and face the unknown alone. Not only do they have the pressure of starting a business, they also have the added weight of explaining (or defending) their decisions to well-intended advice givers. Their personal support network has most likely never started a business before, but will probably try to offer what they think is helpful advice. It may be well-intended advice coming from a place of love, but it won't be the right advice. FGEs need to recognize this, and look to their professional advisors or mentors for direction.

The role of the spouse is important to address again here, as well. Statistically speaking, most spouses don't have experience as an FGE. You and your spouse must have a plan for his/her role in the business, if any, and decide what you are going to communicate and what you will not. This is especially important because your spouse is directly affected by the decisions you make, and the success or failure of the business. Although your spouse might want to help you, he or she often doesn't know how to help and could end up being an unintentional naysayer. This may cause you to feel even more alone.

FGEs who achieve a high level of success often lose control of how others perceive them. Some people may make assumptions or judgments about the FGE based on his or her confidence, assertiveness, risk-taking decisions and all the traits that make him or her a successful entrepreneur. They may assume that all FGEs want to be leaders and in control of every situation. It's entirely possible (and even more likely) that an FGE *won't* want to make decisions outside of work. They may just want to relax, be a "guest," and let someone else take the initiative while on vacation or at non-business-related events.

I've experienced this myself on several occasions. For example, Denise and Dennis, our good friends and fellow FGEs, invited us to their house for dinner. We asked if we could bring something, but they would not take us up on our offer. They were going to wait on us all evening and we would not have to make a single decision. We were going to be their guests and they would take care of everything. We had a phenomenal time enjoying their company, just relaxing and having fun. They understand the challenges of being an FGE, and knew I needed a night "off" from making decisions. I really appreciated that, because it is a rare occurrence.

On another evening, our good friend Brad, also an FGE, treated us to a nice dinner out. He wanted to do this for me because he knows I don't get entertained very often. We enjoyed a delicious meal, and had a great evening laughing, talking and catching up. It was nice for me to have a break from planning the events of the night—and he made me feel like a king. Denise, Dennis and Brad understand what it's like to be an FGE, so they gave me the opportunity to be a guest. Too few people really understand that occasional need.

FGEs may appreciate a break from decision-making on the home front too. So often spouses think they are being accommodating by asking the FGE what he/she wants to do for fun over the weekend, where they want to take the next vacation or where they want to eat on Saturday night. After making decisions at work all day, I personally enjoy not having to make them at home. I often don't have a preference about where to go and what to do, or what to have for dinner. I would rather let someone else in the family take the lead. When those decisions are made for me, I feel pampered, relaxed and can more fully enjoy my time at home.

This is a conversation I have with many FGEs. You often are entertaining clients, directing employees, hosting events and always having to be "on." So many people around you want **you** to make decisions because you are good at making decisions. It's a welcome change to be a guest sometimes. Spouses and non-FGEs may not realize this, so it's important to make your feelings known. It's a small gift they can give you that means a lot.

Some people may assume that FGEs have political opinions primarily rooted around economics and profitability, but that's not necessarily true. There are a lot of dynamics entrepreneurs are faced with from a political or social standpoint. The needs of the business may influence an FGE's support of certain political programs or initiatives. For example, policies around tax cuts may be less important to the FGE than policies around immigration because many businesses need access to laborers. Conscientious capitalism is becoming a bigger part of political thinking. There are politics around retail locations providing bathrooms for people who identify with a different gender. Business owners have to consider the inclusion dynamic while also considering costs.

Non-FGEs will make assumptions about you because they don't understand what it's like to be one. Those assumptions may be untrue or even have a negative undercurrent to them. An FGE develops tough skin fast, but getting there can be disheartening and bothersome. You can't control what other people think of you or say about you; you will have to learn to manage your success and let the assumptions people make roll off your back.

At Gerber, we understand the challenges of FGEs more than most, and have built our entire business around helping them achieve their personal and business goals. We help our clients find clarity about their wants, needs, concerns and hopes.

> At Gerber, we understand the challenges of FGEs more than most, and have built our entire business around helping them achieve their personal and business goals.

We assist them as they visualize their end destination and develop a path to get there. We give them the support they need to fulfill their dreams and keep them moving in the right direction no matter what surprises come their way. And we counsel them holistically on ways they can integrate their business and personal lives, brainstorm planned experience sharing ideas and make everything gel.

For FGEs in the early stages of business, we offer a program called the Emerging Entrepreneur Experience (EEE). EEE is a 12-month program consisting of nine half-day structured sessions with a small group of like-minded entrepreneurs. We provide one-on-one forums; an online portal for presentations, resources and materials; and open office hours with our EEE experts. We offer practical advice and valuable tools that teach FGEs how to work on their business instead of in it.

As a fellow FGE, I would encourage you to seek out and partner with a business advisor or management practice that really understands your challenges. Someone who has been through the stages of business success, came out living to tell about it and is leading the life he or she has always hoped for.

Looking back on my journey as an entrepreneur, there is very little I would change. Writing this book helped me to be part of the innovation process of entrepreneurs—not just their business innovation, but their personal innovation as well. As you may remember from Chapter 1, this is both my personal and professional WHY. The one consistent priority in my life has always been relationships. Relationships are everything. I'm not a "thing" person who prioritizes material items. I'm only an "experience" person if I can have those experiences—a vacation, round of golf or dinner out—with someone else. Bridging my entrepreneurial life with my personal life has been key to my own happiness and success. I'm living my WHY, and it's my hope for you that you will live yours.

KEY TAKEAWAYS

Chapter 1

- Simon Sinek says that success is found when you identify your WHY—the purpose, cause or belief that motivates you to do what you do. Most companies focus on the WHAT or HOW, but the WHY is what separates successful entrepreneurs from the rest.

- As FGEs, we are job creators and the first to do something our own way. We've founded our businesses, defended our views and have lived our lives the way we wanted.

- FGEs are visionary. We see possibilities that others don't and work to make them happen. These opportunities generate wealth, create jobs and grow economies.

- Thanks to former visionaries, we have technologies and conveniences that are a part of our everyday lives. The light bulb, the automobile, the iPhone, and the ability to search any topic on Google to have our questions answered are just a few examples of how early entrepreneurs have changed our world.

- FGEs think differently. We have a much higher need for achievement than non-entrepreneurs; and we value unique, innovative experiences. We EXPECT to succeed. We are passionate, persistent and determined, and are willing to make sacrifices for the sake of our mission.

- Research conducted by Carl Robinson, Ph.D. says successful entrepreneurs share five personality characteristics. Understanding what these are and how they attribute to success can help aspiring or struggling entrepreneurs get back on track.

- FGEs don't view their failures as failures, but as opportunities to learn from past mistakes. We use the knowledge gained to make better and more experienced decisions the next time around.

- Relationships are a crucial part of an FGEs' success. The relationships with people you care about most—your spouse, children, parents and closest friends—will change and grow as your business evolves. Planned experience sharing will enable you to have the utmost satisfaction in all areas of your life.

Chapter 2

- Most entrepreneurs—especially when they are first starting out—struggle to maintain a healthy work-life relationship. The pressure and stress of starting a new business can result in health issues, sleep deprivation, cognitive decline, and conflicts with your spouse, family and friends.

- Instead of working more, we advise our clients to (1) focus only on what moves them forward, (2) develop a plan and stick to it, (3) take scheduled time away to relax and recharge, (4) exercise, and (5) be mindful of alcohol use.

- Integration is making a conscious decision to merge the most important people and events in your life whenever possible.

- Invest your precious time with lifelong, unconditional friends—the ones who are there for you through anything and invest their time back into you.

- Find the kind of integration that works best for you based on how you like to spend your time and who you want to spend it with.

- Planned experience sharing is part of the integration process, and to implement it, you must live deliberately.

- There are six questions you should ask yourself when making deliberate choices and integrating your life: (1) What aspects of your life are most important? (2) What aspects of your life are least important but still suck out your energy? (3) Where do you want to be in your personal and professional life in various points in the future? (4) What do you need to do to move toward your goals? (5) What should you stop doing now to ensure you meet your goals? (6) How do you measure or chart your progress?

- Integrating your life and learning to plan deliberately are the keys to success, both personally and in business.

Chapter 3

- Planned experience sharing is one of an entrepreneur's strongest tools for success in business and life. It allows you to share the time that you would normally split between your work, family, and personal lives.

- The key to planned experience sharing is to consider what you do for a living, where you live, and what your family loves to do. Then determine how you can combine them all in an experience that allows you to network with business associates while spending time with your family.

- Planned experience sharing removes the stress and burden that goes along with trying to wear too many hats too often. It's important to delegate responsibilities to a team member to take some of the work off of your plate and to allow them to grow and develop within their careers.

- To help delegate responsibility and establish accountability, I recommend investing in or at least learning about a business system such as the Entrepreneurial Operating System, Rockefeller Habits, or MAP Management Consulting.

- Only do the things you are world class at doing. Delegate everything else to others. This will leave you less stressed, more productive and able to enjoy those planned, shared experiences.

Chapter 4

- There are three main elements that increase your new business's odds of making it to the second year: timing, idea inspiration and support network.

- In order for your business to be a success, you must consider economical timing, technological timing, political timing and personal timing.

- Ideas are often inspired in the most counterintuitive places, like the shower, the subway or while you are on vacation. They are also inspired while working as an employee in your industry, or as a result of education, willpower and intense industry analysis.

- A solid support network—both formal and informal—is crucial to the success of an entrepreneur.

- Align your business with powerhouse companies such as Google, Amazon and Apple. They can provide your business with a wide variety of business solutions.

- The most important sources of support for first-generation entrepreneurs are immediate family members and close friends. Take solace in the relationships that support you, but be wary of advice given by naysayers.

Chapter 5

- The Intoxicating Stage is the first stage of business success. It's exciting, exhilarating and all consuming.

- Most entrepreneurs never make it out of this stage. If you want to grow your business, you will need the support of your family and your business network.

- Surround yourself with a supportive business network, even if it means you have to form it yourself. Look to successful entrepreneurs to serve as mentors.

- It's vitally important that you don't allow naysayers to let you doubt yourself. Some of the most influential people from a variety of industries have faced naysayers and succeeded despite them.

- When naysayers are people close to you, it can be especially difficult. They love you and want to help, but often don't understand and don't know how to support you. You can't listen to what they say.

Chapter 6

- During the Trapped Stage, the entrepreneur's enthusiasm begins to fade as the realities of owning a business really set in.

- Many entrepreneurs feel trapped financially but forge ahead because they don't want to face their naysayers if the business doesn't work out.

- Failure at this point affects the lives of others and entrepreneurs feel they are no longer in control.

- The Trapped Stage causes high levels of stress, financial pressures, contributes to poor health and places significant strains on personal relationships.

- To get through this stage, entrepreneurs need to revisit their core values, and consult with lawyers, business consulting firms, therapists, or business coaches on how to make smart decisions and overcome stress.

- Maintaining a consistent exercise schedule through the Trapped Stage increases stamina, improves mood, and lowers stress hormones to help you feel focused, calm and relaxed.

Chapter 7

- Entrepreneurs in the Light at the End of the Tunnel stage feel a sense of relief, as they begin to see enough demand for their product or service.

- A business in this stage is still on delicate ground, and may succumb to short-term, temporary failures, bad decisions or bad luck.

- To succeed, entrepreneurs must learn to work "on" their business instead of "in" their business and accept being a leader in spirit, not in form.

- A consultant, mentor or advisory board can view your business and your business's goals through new perspectives and backgrounds.

- Implementing a management system such as EOS, MAP Management Consulting and Rockefeller Habits helps ensure you'll make fewer mistakes and improves the odds of your success.

- Entrepreneurs in the Light at the End of the Tunnel Stage now have more time and money to establish good work-life habits using integration and planned experience sharing.

Chapter 8

- Businesses that enter the Acceleration Stage are clearly moving forward. They can now invest more in their leadership team, their benefits program and further develop their employer-employee relationships.

- To make it through this stage, the entrepreneur must transition from employee owner to investor owner.

- Short-term failures still occur at this stage, but they aren't as likely to derail the business as they were in earlier stages.

- A business must embrace innovation in order to grow. This can be disruptive and uncomfortable, but entrepreneurs must innovate to take their business to the next level.

- While innovation is crucial, it should not consume all of your time. Maintain relationships with those in your personal life.

- The Acceleration Stage is the first big opportunity you will have to carve out the tasks that aren't productive, and focus on what is core to your personal and business mission.

- Entrepreneurs in this stage should hire personal managers to further accelerate growth. It can be difficult for most entrepreneurs to let go of this part of the business, but it's necessary in order to move on to Stage Five.

Chapter 9

- Reaching the Sustainable Stage is a huge accomplishment, but entrepreneurs must not let their confidence turn into arrogance or complacency. They need to lay the foundation for permanence and longevity, and put evergreen solutions in place.

- To succeed, a business must know its limitations and be very deliberate about its actions.

- The entrepreneur in the Sustainable Stage must change his or her relationship with the business, and become the investor owner instead of the employee owner.

- Many entrepreneurs cycle through the five stages more than once as their business faces new challenges and opportunities.

- If integration and planned experience sharing were prioritized as entrepreneurs went through the stages, the foundation will be laid for both by the time they reach Stage Five.

- If an entrepreneur has not successfully prioritized the relationships outside of business, it's never too late to start new habits and redefine what's important to them.

Chapter 10

- Good business practices can help the entrepreneur avoid temporary failures and the impact of them.

- Develop a written business plan that can be adjusted as your customers' needs change, but that remain aligned with your vision.

- Be flexible and open minded to opportunities you did not anticipate.

- Know your competition and how your product or service is different or better.

- Listen to your advisors, not your naysayers.

- Take steps to protect your emotional and financial resources from temporary failures.

- As challenging as starting a business can be, keep a positive attitude, stay motivated and most importantly, have fun.

- Temporary failures are something to be learned from and are often the steppingstones to success. Permanent failures occur when the entrepreneur has lost enthusiasm and a drive to persevere, cannot find the lesson in failure and does not have the emotional or financial resources to start again.

Chapter 11

- The relationship between an entrepreneur, the spouse, and the business is complicated and extremely important. It contributes to the success of both the business and the marriage, or their demise.

- Entrepreneurs can make both their marriage and their business thrive by implementing a marriage integration plan.

- The first step in the marriage integration plan is communication. Determine how much your spouse wants to know about the business.

- The second step in the marriage integration plan is to determine your shared and competing personal goals. Spend some time discussing your relationship, how to nurture it and the kind of life you want to live.

- The third step in the marriage integration plan is to determine the spouse's role in the business. If you decide together that your spouse will be involved, his or her position should always evolve and adapt to what is best for the business and the marriage.

- As discussed in earlier chapters, planned experience sharing is scheduling time to focus on your marriage when you can be completely present and emotionally available. Also schedule time to talk about the business, such as during a planned weekly check-in. It's important to do this through all the stages of business.

Chapter 12

- Having an entrepreneurial parent teaches children valuable life lessons about problem solving, confidence, creativity, empowerment, imagination and independence.

- Families today differ in structure, but managing parental and work roles is harder than it's ever been in the US, and entrepreneurial parents are exceptionally overextended.

- The key to a supportive, happy family lies in deliberately planning how you spend your time in order to serve your current needs and your goals for the future.

- Since you'll often have to respond to the changing needs of your business and your children at the same time, you must practice conscious communication and planned experience sharing.

- Your children will need you in different ways as they grow, and it's important to adjust how and when you interact with them as they go through their childhood stages.

- As your business grows and you have more time and money, be deliberate in creating meaningful family experiences.

Chapter 13

- Research shows that children of entrepreneurial parents are 60 percent more likely to be entrepreneurs themselves. Conflicts/problems with their parents will still arise, but the child entrepreneur usually feels understood.

- Parents of FGEs almost always told their child to get a "real job" for stability, at least at first.

- The FGE's quest to make their parents understand their decision becomes one of his/her greatest struggles.

- If you can, get your parents involved with your plans by inviting them to business launch parties, networking events and company outings.

- You must be able to stay focused and motivated despite your unintentional naysayer parents. Hear their criticisms, know they only want what's best for you, but continue to build the life you want the way you want it.

Chapter 14

- Having two or three unconditional friends can have a wildly profound and positive impact on your life. Use planned experience sharing to integrate them into your life.

- Through your entrepreneurial journey, you may discover that your best friends are other FGEs who understand the challenges and pressures of starting a business.

- If you decide to mix business with friendship, determine what role you want that person to play in your business, articulate clear expectations and have an exit strategy. Do this whether your friend will be your employee or an investor in your company.

- In my experience, most business partnerships between friends don't work, and there are messy breakups because there is no exit strategy.

- Understand that hiring a friend will change your friendship, but the arrangement can be successful if you work out as many potential issues and problems as possible before the relationship commences.

DISCUSSION QUESTIONS

Chapter 1: How Entrepreneurs Are Different

1. Have you defined your business's WHY? If so, explain what it is and how you chose it. If you haven't, what's holding you back? Ask yourself WHY you are doing what you do.

2. What are your business's core values, and how do they support your WHY?

3. How have you been a "Visionary" in your business?

4. FGEs think about the world differently than everyone else. How have you used your unique thinking and perspective to grow your business?

5. How does your approach to business differ from the non-entrepreneurs you know? Do you set extremely high

expectations for those around you? Are you afraid to delegate responsibilities for fear they won't "do it like you do"? Discuss why you feel that way.

6. FGEs value success and value themselves more highly when they believe they have achieved it. How do you feel about yourself when you achieve something significant in your business? How do you feel about yourself when something in your business fails?

7. Rate yourself according to Carl Robinson's five personality characteristics—emotional intelligence, optimism, tolerance for frustration, tolerance for criticism, and self control. Which characteristics do you excel at? Which characteristics do you need to work on?

Chapter 2: Why Integrate?

1. Time is a valuable resource, and FGEs never have enough of it. How successful have you been with integrating your work and personal life? After reading this chapter, what could you do differently to merge these two parts of your life more effectively?

2. How much sleep do you get each night? Do you feel it's enough? Think about your evening routine and assess if it's working for you. What could you change to give yourself the rest time your body/mind needs?

3. When is the last time you reviewed your written business plan? If you haven't set eyes on it in a while or don't have one, what steps will you take to be sure this gets completed and reviewed regularly?

4. When you pull yourself away from your business and view it from a different lens, what do you see? Do you like what you see? How often do you take the time to do this?

5. Think about your unconditional friends. How can you deliberately invest more of your time, emotions and energy in them, and less into your conditional friends or acquaintances?

6. How successful have you been at measuring your task list against your goals for the future? Are you managing your to-do list, or is it managing you? How can you be better at this?

Chapter 3: Planned Experience Sharing

1. What activities, hobbies, or organizations do you enjoy most? How could these be incorporated into planned experience sharing so you can fully integrate your work and personal lives?

2. Think about the number of "hats" you wear in your business. How effective are you at delegating? Which of these "hats" do you dislike, and could be passed on to someone who enjoys doing them?

3. Does your business have a management system—like EOS, Rockefeller Habits, or MAP Management Consulting? If so, how is it working for you? If you don't, what's holding you back?

4. What tasks are you "world class" at doing? What steps can you take to make sure that's where you spend your time, and delegate everything else?

Chapter 4: Defining Success

1. Did your business enter your industry at the "right" time? What kind of research did you conduct to understand that

the market was ready for your product or service? How many times did you fail before you got the timing right?

2. Think about what inspired you to start your business. How did you come up with the idea? Was it by accident, while you were at work, or a result of intense industry analysis?

3. What support groups are you a part of? How have they helped you grow your business?

4. What are your favorite business tools or apps that you couldn't live without? (Think GSuite, Amazon, Slack, Zoom, etc.) What impact have they had on your business?

5. How did your immediate family members and close friends react when you told them you wanted to start your own business? Have you gained anything from their insights? Are they supportive, or is there a naysayer among them?

Chapter 5: Stage One —The Intoxicating Stage

1. Think about your business's intoxicating stage. What was it like for you? Are you still in it?

2. What support group(s) did you have in this stage? Did you lean on your peers, a mentor or an advisory board? Discuss whether you got what you needed from your support network, and if you'd make any changes if you had to do it all over again.

3. Reflecting back on the examples of U2 and Harper Lee, how many times did you have to go back to the drawing board before your idea got traction?

4. Who is the "Mike" in your life, and how have you handled him? Is your "Mike" an intentional or unintentional naysayer?

5. What steps have you taken to surround yourself with people who are positive, supportive and realistic?

Chapter 6: Stage Two—The Trapped Stage

1. If you've been there, describe what it was like to enter your business's Trapped Stage. What sent you there? Was it one situation, or a series of events? If you're not there yet, have you anticipated what could lead you there?

2. How does the Trapped Stage affect an FGE's health? Eating habits? Stress level? How did you manage through yours?

3. Do you make time to exercise during your business's stressful times, or is it the first thing to go? How has exercise (or lack of it) affected your ability to move forward?

4. What are some possible financial risks, employee risks and/ or business risks needed to get past this stage?

5. Hindsight is 20/20. If you've experienced the Trapped Stage, what lessons did you learn from it, and what would you handle differently?

Chapter 7: Stage Three—The Light at the End of the Tunnel Stage

1. How did you feel when you entered the Light at the End of the Tunnel Stage—was there a sense of relief? Anxiety? Apprehension? Enthusiasm? If you're not there yet, how do you imagine you will feel?

2. How can you shift from working "in" your business to working "on" your business? What tasks can you delegate to someone else?

3. FGEs in this stage "don't know what they don't know." Who do you turn to for strategic advice?

4. Have you used a business management system? If so, which one was it, and did it work for you? If you haven't, how can you educate yourself about running your business more efficiently?

5. How can you incorporate integration and planned experience sharing into this stage? If you have already done so, were you successful? What could you have done better?

Chapter 8: Stage Four—The Acceleration Stage

1. Businesses that enter the Acceleration Stage make improvements like building their leadership teams, expanding their benefits program, and developing policy and procedures. What improvements can you make in your business during this stage, and why?

2. How can you manage stress, integration and planned experience sharing during the Acceleration Stage?

3. How have you transitioned from "employee owner" to "investor owner"? What growing pains came along with that? If you haven't done it yet, define the steps you will need to take to begin working "on" your business instead of "in" it.

4. How has your business innovated or "reinvented itself" in order to stay afloat?

5. What are your goals in each area of your life (business, family, friends, etc.) over the next 10, 20 or 25 years? What do you need to do in the next 90 days to achieve those goals?

6. Has your business hired a professional manager? Why or why not? If you have, what has your experience been?

Chapter 9: Stage Five—The Sustainable Stage

1. How is experiencing the Sustainable Stage (the last of the five stages) similar to experiencing the Intoxicating Stage (the first of the five stages)? How is it different?

2. How can a business nurture and invest in itself to ensure it will thrive and not fail?

3. Restaurants like Pasquale's and White Castle succeeded while others like Burger Chef and Cooker did not, primarily because its owners changed the relationship with their businesses. How has your relationship with your business changed? Are you a full "investor owner"?

4. The five stages of business success are fluid. How many times have you been through all or parts of the process? Do you expect to go through all or parts of it again?

5. If you have made it to Stage Five, are you a master of integration and planned experience sharing? Or is your mastery a work in progress?

Chapter 10: Strategies to Avoid the Impact of Failure

1. What temporary failures have you experienced in your business? How did you handle them, and what did you learn from them?

2. How has your business plan changed with each stage of your business growth? Do you know where your business is going?

THE INTEGRATED ENTREPRENEUR

3. How adaptable is your business plan? Do you have the ability to be flexible as new ideas and opportunities present themselves?

4. How well do you understand your competition? How is your business unique and different from everyone else? How do you research your competition?

5. Describe a time when you overpromised something to a client or customer. Were you able to deliver? If not, how did you handle it? How did the client or customer react? What did you learn?

6. Sometimes having fun while running a business requires deliberate and intentional effort. How good are you at unplugging from work and making time for fun? Where could you improve?

7. John C. Maxwell, author of *Failing Forward*, said that the only people who will succeed are the people who have had a positive attitude toward failure. Think about a time when you experienced a temporary failure. Did you view it as a personal failure or a learning experience? Did it make you want to be better, or give up?

8. Have you ever experienced a permanent failure or know someone who has? How do you keep your temporary failures from becoming permanent ones?

Chapter 11: Marriage

1. Have you and your spouse established good communication habits, such as a weekly check-in? How did you and your spouse decide when, where and how much you would communicate about the business?

2. What kind of life do you and your spouse want to live? Have you talked about your goals—such as the house you

want to live in, vacations you want to take, or the number of kids you want to have?

3. How do you set aside time for just you and your spouse where you don't talk about the business? How often does that happen? Is it enough?

4. What role does your spouse have in your business, if any? Is your arrangement working for your marriage and your business?

5. How have you used planned experience sharing in your marriage?

Chapter 12: Children

1. As an FGE, you are modeling focus and drive for your children. How do you show them what it means to be a confident, hard-working, independent thinker?

2. How satisfied are you with your work and family integration efforts? When you are home, do you feel you are emotionally available to them?

3. How has the time spent with your children changed as they have gotten older?

4. Have you spent time with your child at your office, or included them in any family-friendly networking or work events? How did they react to seeing you in this environment?

5. How do you plan for spending time with your children, away from work and without thinking about work?

6. How have you incorporated planned experience sharing into the time spent with your children? What opportunities do you have coming up that you could utilize this practice?

Chapter 13: Parents

1. How did your parents react when you told them you wanted to start your own business? Were they happy? Supportive? Nervous? Did they encourage you to follow your dream, or "get a real job?"

2. Was it important to you to have your parents' understanding or approval about starting your own business? Why or why not?

3. Did their initial feelings about your business change as the years went by?

4. When reflecting on your parents' reaction to your desire to start a business, has it changed how you parent your own children and prepare them for their futures? If so, how?

Chapter 14: Friends

1. Time is a precious commodity, and you need to invest in people who are willing to invest in you. Which of your friends are always there for you with a word of encouragement or a new perspective?

2. Did your relationship with your non-entrepreneur friends change after you started your business? If so, how?

3. How have you used integration and planned experience sharing to keep in touch with your unconditional friends?

4. Do any of your friends play a role in your business—either as an investor, a partner or an employee? Did you discuss the details and lay the groundwork first, or jump right in? How did it work out?

ENDNOTES

1   Simon Sinek, *Start with Why: How Great Leaders Inspire Everyone to Take Action* (Penguin Group, 2009).

2   Saras Sarasvathy. (2008). University of Virginia Darden School of Business study. *What Makes Entrepreneurs Entrepreneurial?* Retrieved from https://www.effectuation.org/sites/default/files/research_papers/what-makes-entrepreneurs-entrepreneurial-sarasvathy_0.pdf

3   EO Entrepreneurs Organization. *EO Global Entrepreneur Indicator, U.S. Edition, September 2017.* Retrieved from https://www.eonetwork.org/global-entrepreneur-indicator/Download%20Reports/September%202017/GEI_One%20Pager_Sept%202017_v2_US.pdf

4   Barb Darrow. (February 2017). *Why It's a Good Time to Start Your Own Company.* Fortune Magazine. Retrieved from https://fortune.com/2017/02/22/startups-2017-challenger/

5   Steve Jobs. (June 2005). *Stanford Commencement Address*. Retrieved from https://news.stanford.edu/2005/06/14/jobs-061505/ https://www.youtube.com/watch?v=D1R-jKKp3NA

6   Kenneth Benston. (September 2018). *US Capital Markets in 2018*. SIFMA News. Retrieved from https://www.sifma.org/resources/news/us-capital-markets-in-2018/

7   Jason Wiens and Chris Jackson. (September 2015). *The Importance of Young Firms for Economic Growth*. Ewing Marion Kauffman Foundation. Retrieved from http://www.kauffman.org/what-we-do/resources/entrepreneurship-policy-digest/the-importance-of-young-firms-for-economic-growth

8   Scott S. Smith. (April 2016). *Cyrus McCormick Revolutionized Farming Worldwide With the Reaper. Investor's Business Daily.* Retrieved from https://www.investors.com/news/management/leaders-and-success/cyrus-mccormick-revolutionized-farming-worldwide-with-the-reaper/

9   biography.com (June 2019). *Andrew Carnegie Biography.* Retrieved from https://www.biography.com/people/andrew-carnegie

10 Tim Bajarin (June 2017). *How Apple's iPhone Changed These 5 Major Industries*. Time. Retrieved from http://time.com/4832599/iphone-anniversary-industry-change/

11 Carl J. Schamm PhD, *The Entrepreneurial Imperative*. (Harper Business, 2013).

12 James Goodnight, co-founder of SAS (Statistical Analysis Software) Institute, Inc. quotes. Retrieved from https://www.sas.com/en_us/company-information/leadership/jim-goodnight.html

13 Fortune 100 Best (August 2019). *SAS Company Review.* Fortune. Retrieved from: https://fortune.com/best-companies/2019/sas-institute

14 Georgia McIntyre (September 2019). *What Percentage of Small Businesses Fail?* fundera.com blog. Retrieved from https://www.fundera.com/blog/what-percentage-of-small-businesses-fail

15 Patrick Henry (February 2017). *Why Some Startups Succeed (and Why Most Fail).* Entrepreneur. Retrieved from https://www.entrepreneur.com/article/288769

16 John C. Maxwell. *Failing Forward: Turning Mistakes Into Stepping Stones for Success.* (Thomas Nelson, 2000).

17 Student/entrepreneur quote. Retrieved from https://dukeo.com/entrepreneurship-is-living-a-few-years-of-your-life-like-most-people-wont-so-that-you-can-spend/

18 Cardiff Garcia (January 2011). *Mortal Magnates.* Association for Psychological Science. Retrieved from https://www.psychologicalscience.org/observer/mortal-magnates-research-shows-entrepreneurs-are-pretty-much-like-the-rest-of-us

19 Cardiff Garcia (January 2011). *Mortal Magnates.* Association for Psychological Science. Retrieved from https://www.psychologicalscience.org/observer/mortal-magnates-research-shows-entrepreneurs-are-pretty-much-like-the-rest-of-us

20 entrepreneurshiptheories.blogspot (April 2019) *What is the Achievement Motivation Theory of Entrepreneurship?* Retrieved from https://entrepreneurshiptheories.blogspot.com/2017/08/need-for-achievement-achievement.html

21 Carl Robinson, PhD (cited by Mary Sullivan in allbusiness.com). *How Are Entrepreneurs Different?* Retrieved from https://www.allbusiness.com/entrepreneurs-are-not-like-normal-folk-2-8698936-1.html

22 Gallup Poll (December 2013). *In U.S., 40% Get Less Than Recommended Amount of Sleep.* Retrieved from https://news.gallup.com/poll/166553/less-recommended-amount-sleep.aspx

23 Whitehall II Study Findings (March 2009). *Long Working Hours and Cognitive Function.* U.S. National Library of Medicine. Retrieved from https://www.ncbi.nlm.nih.gov/pubmed/19126590

24 Robert Sapolsky, *Why Zebras Don't Get Ulcers.* (Henry Holt and Company, LLC. 2004).

25 Business Plan Templates. Retrieved from SCORE, https://www.score.org/resource/business-plan-template-startup-business; the U.S. Small Business Administration, https://www.sba.gov/tools/business-plan/1; and Entrepreneur magazine, https://www.entrepreneur.com/article/247574

26 Sherrie Campbell (May 2017). *12 Habits of Highly Effective Entrepreneurs.* Entrepreneur. Retrieved from https://www.entrepreneur.com/article/294080

27 Spencer Blackman (October 2015). *Working Too Much, Drinking Too Much.* Entrepreneur. Retrieved from https://www.entrepreneur.com/article/251189

28 Gallup Poll (March 2018). *Most Small Business Owners Don't Plan to "Fully" Retire.* Retrieved from https://news.gallup.com/poll/104866/four-smallbusiness-owners-dont-plan-retire.aspx

29 Entrepreneurs' Organization. Retrieved from http://www.eonetwork.org/

30 Entrepreneurial Operating System®. Retrieved from http://eosworldwide.com

31 Verne Harnish. *Mastering the Rockefeller Habits: What You Must Do to Increase the Value of Your Growing Firm.* (Select Books, Inc., 2002). Retrieved from https://www.amazon.com/Mastering-Rockefeller-Habits-Increase-ebook/dp/B005J386GS

32 MAP Vital Factors Solutions. Retrieved from https://www.mapconsulting.com

33 Paul Gompers, Anna Kovner, Josh Lerner and David Scharfstein (April 2010). *Performance Persistence in Entrepreneurship. Journal of Financial Economics.* Retrieved from https://www.hbs.edu/faculty/Pages/item.aspx?num=37618

34 Grant and funding sources for energy efficiency and renewable energy technologies. Retrieved from the Small Business Innovation Research (SBIR) program, https://www.sbir.gov; the Small Business Technology Transfer program, https://www.nsf.gov/funding/pgm_summ.jsp?pims_id=505362 and the Advance Research Projects Agency-Energy (ARPA-E) program, https://arpa-e.energy.gov

35 Latham & Watkins Report No. 827 (March 2009). *American Recovery and Reinvestment Act of 2009—Implications for Cleantech Companies and Investment.* Retrieved from https://www.lw.com/thoughtLeadership/implications-of-arra-for-cleantech

36 Tesla – Statistics & Facts (September 2019). Retrieved from https://www.statista.com/topics/2086/tesla/

37 Colleen Connolly (August 2013). *How the Coffee Cup Sleeve Was Invented.* Retrieved from https://www.smithsonianmag.com/arts-culture/how-the-coffee-cup-sleeve-was-invented-119479/

38 Raffi Amit (November 2009). *How Entrepreneurs Identify New Business Opportunities.* Wharton University of Pennsylvania. Retrieved from http://knowledge.wharton.upenn.edu/article/how-entrepreneurs-identify-new-business-opportunities/

39 Arnobio Morelix (October 2015). *The evolution of entrepreneurship on college campuses – a timeline.* Ewing Marion Kauffman Foundation. Retrieved from https://www.kauffman.org/blogs/growthology/2015/10/the-evolution-of-entrepreneurship-on-college-campuses

40 Keenan Center for Entrepreneurship, The Ohio State University Fisher College of Business. Retrieved from https://fisher.osu.edu/centers-partnerships/cie

41 The Ohio State University Fisher College of Business. *Undergraduate Entrepreneurship & Innovation Minor.* Retrieved from https://files.fisher.osu.edu/undergraduate/public/entrepreneurship_innovation_minor_v1.0.pdf

42 Small Business Development Centers (SBDC). Retrieved from https://www.sba.gov/tools/local-assistance/sbdc

43 John C. Maxwell. *Failing Forward: Turning Mistakes Into Stepping Stones for Success.* (Thomas Nelson, 2000).

44 Retrieved from https://www.startupamericapartnership.org/

45 Gsuite Tools. Retrieved from https://gsuite.google.com/features/

46 Google My Business. Retrieved from https://www.google.com/business/

47 Amazon Business Features. Retrieved from https://www.amazon.com/b2b/info/features?layout=landing

48 Apple Small Business. Retrieved from https://www.apple.com/retail/business/

49 U2 The Band. Retrieved from http://www.u2.com/band

50 Harper Lee quote (September 1961). Writer's Digest. Retrieved from https://www.goodreads.com/quotes/939628-i-would-advise-anyone-who-aspires-to-a-writing-career

51 Dave Ghose (June 2008). *The final days of Skybus.* Columbus Monthly. Retrieved from http://www.columbusmonthly.com/content/stories/2010/02/the-final-days-of-skybus.html

52 Jack Chua (September 2017). *6 Companies That Failed To Make It Through The 'Middle Mile.'* Leaderonomics.

Retrieved from https://leaderonomics.com/business/
failed-businesses-middle-mile

53 Jessica Bruder (2014). The Psychological Price of
Entrepreneurship. Inc. Retrieved from https://www.inc.
com/magazine/201309/jessica-bruder/psychological-price-
of-entrepreneurship.html

54 Moe Kittaneh (April 2017). *7 Reasons Every Entrepreneur
Should Start the Day With Exercise.* Entrepreneur. Retrieved
from https://www.entrepreneur.com/article/290436

55 Kimberly Amadeo (May 2019; updated). *2008 Financial
Crisis ... The Causes and Costs of the Worst Crisis Since the
Great Depression.* Retrieved from https://www.thebalance.
com/2008-financial-crisis-3305679

56 The Spot Athletics. Retrieved from https://www.
thespotathletics.com

57 Instant Pot. Retrieved from https://www.nytimes.com/2017/
12/17/business/instant-pot.html

58 Balani Custom Clothes. Retrieved from https://www.
balanicustom.com/about-us/#

59 Walmart Staff (February 2018). *Take a Trip Through 50
Years of Retail Innovation.* Retrieved from https://blog.
walmart.com/innovation/20180201/take-a-trip-through-
50-years-of-retail-innovation

60 Chris Isidore. (March 2018). *Amazon didn't kill Toys 'R' Us.
Here's what did.* CNN Business. Retrieved from https://money.
cnn.com/2018/03/15/news/companies/toys-r-us-closing-
blame/index.html?iid=EL

61 Scott D. Anthony. (July 2016). *Kodak's Downfall Wasn't About
Technology.* Harvard Business Review. Retrieved from https://
hbr.org/2016/07/kodaks-downfall-wasnt-about-technology

62 Pasquale's. Retrieved from http://www.pasquales.com

63 Kate Kelly. (June 2015). *White Castle Hamburgers: The Story*. America Comes Alive. Retrieved from https://americacomesalive. com/2015/06/15/white-castle-hamburgers-the-story/

64 Jonathan Maze. (2014). *Five Chains That Suffered Spectacular Designs*. Restaurant Finance Monitor. Retrieved from http:// www.restfinance.com/Restaurant-Finance-Across-America/ March-2014/Five-Chains-That-Suffered-Spectacular-Declines/

65 Laura Newpoff. (April 2004). *Cooker restaurant chain 'is no more'*. Columbus Business First. Retrieved from https://www. bizjournals.com/columbus/stories/2004/04/26/daily24.html

66 Dave Chaffey. (August 2018). *Amazon.com case study – 2018 Update*. Smart Insights. Retrieved from https:// www.smartinsights.com/digital-marketing-strategy/online-business-revenue-models/amazon-case-study/

67 Dara Khosrowshahi. (September 2018). *Uber Raising the Bar on Safety*. Uber Newsroom. Retrieved from https://www.uber. com/newsroom/raisingthebar/

68 Liz Meyerdirk. (October 2018). *Uber Eats Delivers Subway® Sandwiches, Salads and More to Your Door*. Uber News-room. Retrieved from https://www.uber.com/newsroom/ uber-eats-delivers-subway-sandwiches/

69 Rhea Dookeran. (October 2018). *Another way to get from A to B with JUMP Scooters*. Uber Newsroom. Retrieved from https://www.uber.com/newsroom/jump-scooters/

70 Dara Khosrowshahi. (October 2018. Uber Drives the Vote. Uber Newsroom. Retrieved from https://www.uber.com/ newsroom/drivethevote/

71 W. Chan Kim, Renee Mauborgne. *Blue Ocean Strategy* (Harvard Business Review Press, 2015).

72 John C. Maxwell. *Failing Forward: Turning Mistakes Into Stepping Stones for Success*. (Thomas Nelson, 2000).

73 Thomas Koulopoulos. (October 2015). *5 of the Most Surprising Statistics About Startups*. Inc. Retrieved from https://www.inc.com/thomas-koulopoulos/5-of-the-most-surprising-statistics-about-start-ups.html

74 Year On Team. (December 2014). *Overcoming Failure: The Perseverance of Henry Ford*. Year On Blog. Retrieved from https://www.yearon.com/blog/successes-of-henry-ford

75 Meg Cadoux Hirshberg. (September 2013). *Of Drivers and Passengers. Or, How Entrepreneurs' Families Cope*. Inc. Retrieved from http://www.inc.com/magazine/201309/meg-cadoux-hirshberg/meg-hirshbergs-last-balancing-acts-column.html

76 Ellen Galinsky. *Mind in the Making*. (Harper Collins Publishers, 2010).

77 Chyi-lyi Liang, Paul Dunn. (March 2002). *The Impact of Starting a New Venture on the Entrepreneurs and Their Families: Expectations, Reality, and Willingness to Start Again*. Journal of Business and Entrepreneurship. Retrieved from https://www.questia.com/library/journal/1P3-1395129781/the-impact-of-starting-a-new-venture-on-the-entrepreneurs

78 Jamie Doward. (January 2017). *Men and women struggle to get on at work and find time for their families*. The Guardian. Retrieved from https://www.theguardian.com/money/2017/jan/22/fatherhood-penalty-balance-work-family-life-millennial-men

79 Minet Schindehutte, Catriona Brennan, Michael Morris. (January 2003). *Entrepreneurs and Motherhood: Impacts on Their Children in South Africa and the United States. Journal of Small Business Management*. Retrieved from https://www.researchgate.net/

publication/228315028_Entrepreneurs_and_Motherhood_
Impacts_on_Their_Children_in_South_Africa_and_the_
United_States

80 S.A. McLeod. (May 2018). *Erik Erikson's stages of psychosocial development.* Simply Psychology. Retrieved from https://www.simplypsychology.org/Erik-Erikson.html

81 Matthew J. Lindquist, Mirjam van Praag, Joeri Sol. (April 2015). *Why Do Entrepreneurial Parents Have Entrepreneurial Children?* SSRN Electronic Journal. Retrieved from https://www.researchgate.net/publication/254405707_Why_Do_Entrepreneurial_Parents_Have_Entrepreneurial_Children

82 Jeffrey Taylor, Marcia B. Harris, Susan Taylor. (Winter 2004). *Parents Have Their Say ... About Their College-Age Children's Career Decisions.* National Association of Colleges and Employers Journal. Retrieved from https://www.hampshire.edu/sites/default/files/shared_files/Parents_Have_Their_Say.pdf

83 David Levine. (July 2018). *Are Friends the Key to Happiness?* U.S. News. Retrieved from https://health.usnews.com/health-care/patient-advice/articles/2018-07-27/are-friends-the-key-to-happiness

ABOUT THE AUTHOR

Randy Gerber is the founder and advisor of Gerber, LLC., a professional services firm focused solely on improving the business and overall happiness of first-generation entrepreneurs. Gerber, LLC helps their clients integrate, grow their businesses with purpose, and achieve their life, business and financial goals.

Randy is also the founder and advisor of The Emerging Entrepreneur Experience™, a program focused on helping business owners generating less than $2 million in business revenue get on track, stay focused and attain results.

Randy was inspired to write *The Integrated Entrepreneur* after experiencing how integration and planned experience sharing impacted his own personal and business life. Along with Gerber LLC and the Emerging Entrepreneur Experience™, *The Integrated Entrepreneur* contributes to a supportive ecosystem for other first-generation entrepreneurs.

Randy is a graduate of The Ohio State University's Fisher College of Business. He has volunteered at the Childhood League Center, American Heart Association and is an active supporter of

Mid-Ohio Foodbank and Festa. In addition, Randy has been an extremely active member and leader of the Columbus Chapter of the Entrepreneurs Organization, including serving as a board member six times since 2000.

Randy credits much of his company's success to their customized, holistic approach to professional services. He and his team help clients take care of the details and align their business and personal lives, enabling the business owner to focus on growth with purpose—a process that betters themselves, their families, their employees, and, ultimately, the community. He lives in Upper Arlington, Ohio with his wife, Emily; their three children, Zoe, Nikko and George; and their family dog, Edward.

gerber

INTEGRATING LIFE, BUSINESS & WEALTH.

FIRST GENERATION ENTREPRENEURS ARE DIFFERENT
SO OUR PROCESS IS TOO

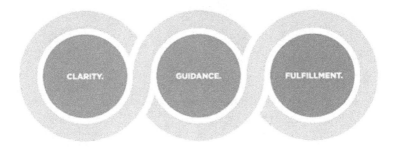

CLARITY. GUIDANCE. FULFILLMENT.

What you get:

Clarity. Finding your WHY and getting you there
Guidance. Creating a plan that integrates your priorities
Fulfillment. Launching your plan and building your legacy

Clearing the path for first generation entrepreneurs to achieve their life, business, and financial goals

READY TO GROW YOUR BUSINESS WITH PURPOSE?

Visit our website at www.GerberClarity.com

EMERGING ENTREPRENEUR EXPERIENCE ™

WE HELP GROWTH-MINDED ENTREPRENEURS BUILD KICK-ASS BUSINESSES AND LIVE HAPPIER LIVES

EEE provides the processes, strategies and sequencing for success. Our successful clients are industry leaders, lead happy + fulfilling lives and make money doing it

What You Get:

Investment in You. Fire yourself from unwanted tasks and focus your efforts on what you do best

Collaboration. Build an ecosystem of FGEs just like you

Wisdom. Curriculum curated from years of experience working with 200+ FGEs

Executable Roadmap. Improve your growth and profitability with strategic, actionable content

JOIN OUR ENTREPRENEUR MOVEMENT TODAY!

Visit our website at www.GerberEmerging.com

CPSIA information can be obtained
at www.ICGtesting.com
Printed in the USA
BVHW010624041021
617751BV00010B/330/J